Number 12

Hot Rodding
INTERNATIONAL

Contents

Front cover photo: Chris and Charise Trombetta's '33 Ford coupe has a long and interesting history. Read all about it, starting on page 170.

Published in 2020 by Graffiti Publications Pty. Ltd.
69 Forest Street, Castlemaine, 3450, Victoria, Australia
Phone International: 61 3 5472 3653 or 61 3 5472 3805.
Email: info@graffitipub.com.au
Website: www.graffitipub.com.au
Publisher/Editor: Larry O'Toole
Text & Production: Larry O'Toole, Al O'Toole, Mary-Anna Brennand
Sales & Marketing: Mary O'Toole, Wendy Thomas
Photos: Larry O'Toole, Al O'Toole, Mary O'Toole, Greg Stokes, Matt Wood, Peter Carpenter, Des Russell.

The information in this publication is true and complete to the best of our knowledge. All recommendations are made without any guarantee on the part of the author or publisher, who also disclaim any liability incurred in connection with the use of this data or specific details.

We recognise that some words, model names and designations mentioned herein, are the property of the trademark holder. We use them for identification purposes only. This is not an official publication.

Graffiti Publications titles are also available at discounts in bulk quantity for industrial or sales promotional use. For details contact Graffiti Publications Ph: (613) 5472 3653. Printed & bound in Singapore by SC (Sang Choy) International Pte Ltd. ISSN: 1836-2850. ISBN: 978-0-949398-45-1

Larry O'Toole

Introduction

Staying the course in a digital world

As this issue of Hot Rodding International went to print, all the talk of the magazine industry was the demise of the TEN (The Enthusiast Network) printed magazines in the USA. Nineteen magazines were chopped from printed production with very little notice and staff stood down accordingly. This knocks a giant hole in the auto enthusiast based magazine publishing world and sent shock-waves through the industry world-wide. As publishers of this magazine and Australian Street Rodding, this change in the landscape will have a knock-on affect, an opportunity to grow for Hot Rodding International and concern for Australian Street Rodding because the distributors of magazines generally now have to contend with a chunk of their business disappearing in a flash. Because Graffiti Publications is a small, family owned business we can adapt to changing technology and market conditions fairly readily, in fact we have done so on more than one occasion in the past. However it is feasible that at some time in the future all printed magazines might have to look at adopting a subscription only model to stay alive.

When we initiated Hot Rodding International as an annual publication back in 2009, we did so with an eye to the role that future technology might play in making it available to a world-wide audience. No, not on making it a digital only product, as the corporate publishers seemed to think was the only future option, but on making use of digital technology to provide a new way to bring printed publications to their audiences. Digital printing is an advancing technology that we sought to take advantage of, but it hasn't progressed at the rate we expected and the cost to produce hasn't fallen as much as we expected it might as the technogy is taken up. In short we anticipated being able to produce the magazine from our offices in Castlemaine, Australia and upload the final files to digital printers all around the world where the finished product could be printed and delivered semi-locally to an international audience. I remain confident that day will come, but in the meantime it is still much more cost-effective to conventionaly print and freight from one central point to our world-wide distribution partners. Being able to print digitally in several locations around the world and deliver locally would be a real bonus as the amount of work and cost involved with the international shipping of printed magazines and books is both frustrating and difficult. Hopefully the whole scene will improve soon, in the meantime enjoy your annual dose of international hot rodding culture. ■

Tri-Five Nationals

SHOEBOX CHEVYS DESCEND ON BOWLING GREEN

Words & Photos: Al & Larry O'Toole

MAIN PIC: Registration day for the Tri-Five Nationals was held at the Bowling Green Airport Holiday Inn and adjacent Convention Centre on Thursday August 8, 2019 and the car parks out front were packed with scores of brilliant Tri-Five Chevys of every description. Heading this line up is Nick Freund's "Sinister" gasser '56 two door sedan with the flip front exposing its tunnel ram equipped big block engine.

ABOVE LEFT: Tri-Five Nomads look particularly attractive from this rear three quarter angle of a bronze and cream '57 example. In the background is a '56 Nomad about to take up its parking spot.

ABOVE RIGHT: An endless parade takes place outside the registration building where we found this bumperless and patina drenched '55 two door sedan making a pass through the parking lot at the Welcome Party.

OPPOSITE ABOVE LEFT: You could live in this one, a '57 four door wagon with rooftop camping unit and SWTPTNA rego plate. Blake Evans from Dallas, Texas is travelling to all 48 lower United States to raise funds for ALS. Go to sweetpatina.com.

OPPOSITE ABOVE RIGHT: We don't often see a soft green '57 Nomad but it certainly looks good on this example owned by Dave Bohler. Under the hood is a potent 427 big block engine.

Needing to fill a few days between the NSRA Street Rod Nationals and Bonneville Speed Week meant the Graffiti team were able to take in the first day of the Tri-Five Nationals in Bowling Green, Kentucky. Thursday August 8 was registration and "Party in the Parking Lot" for the entrants who gathered in the car park of the Airport Holiday Inn and adjacent Convention Centre where registration took place. Also housed in the Convention Centre was an exhibition of Tri-Five Chevy customs that proved very popular with entrants and visitors alike. Here were several well-known customs from the fifties and sixties in living colour right before our eyes. Out in the car park, thousands of the popular Tri-Five Chevys in every state of restoration or customization provided a feast for visitors and photographers from around the world.

The Friday and Saturday of the Tri-Five Nationals was held at Beech Bend Park Dragway where there was drag racing and more display areas for all to enjoy. Alas for us it was time to move on. Bonneville and the lure of another Speed Week was beckoning (see page 180).

ABOVE: Here's a rare one that is claimed to be one of only 96 such wagons built for Government use with solid delivery panel on the left side, wagon windows on the right. Bill and Donna Clark have detailed their wagon to perfection.

ABOVE: Gasser style '55s look menacing when they cruise the parking lot together. The green version is owned by Mike Kramer while Patrick Eason entered the silver example following behind.

BELOW: Anna Brady bought her '55 210 sedan in June '55 for $2257.90 travelled 40,000 miles in it and sold it to the current owner in December 1982.

BELOW: How would you like to drive this home? Silver '56 convertible was the Woody's Hot Rodz built give-away car for the Tri-Five Nationals.

TOP: Maybe not appreciated by the purists but this shortened '56 sedan sure catches your eye. Bob Bockting uses blown 427 big block drive line for an exciting ride!

TOP RIGHT: According to the rego plate this '55 Sports Coupe is powered by a blown engine but no rego sticker means we can't tell you who owns it.

ABOVE: Lots of extra tricks on this '56 GMC van including sedan taillights, Nomad trim strips and slick blue and white paintwork.

BELOW & RIGHT: Dennis Milfeld's custom '56 is a genuine '50s custom now fully refurbished with a 350 engine replacing the orignal 265. The colour is Mexican Purple and the interior white leather. All custom accessories are from other '56 model cars.

ABOVE LEFT: Many readers would recognise this widened and lengthened '57 convertible that was designed by Chip Foose and built by Boyd Coddington. Current owners are Bob and Shawna Talton.

ABOVE RIGHT: Dick Freund owns this extensively shaved and flamed '55 sedan that rolls on chrome wheels and has 350 Chevy engine.

LEFT: "Sick Mad" is the completely restyled and refined '55 Nomad of Jim Alley that was built by Tucci Hot Rods. Some of the features include a '64 Chevy roof skin, tapered front fenders and hood and a one-piece lift up tailgate.

BELOW: A top chop, radical lowering via airbags, spotlights and Packard taillights are just a few of the features of Steve and Nancy Rennick's '55 two door sedan. Bubble skirts, Caddy caps, lakes pipes and a louvered hood finish it off.

ABOVE: The perfect accessory for the rear of your '57 sedan – a '57 Chevy inspired bicycle!

LEFT: Beautiful caramel and cream colour scheme on a '56 210 sedan works a treat. Bob and Sue Darney opted for a small block V8 in the engine bay and complimentary leather interior trim with ostrich leather inserts.

RIGHT: Ronnie E Jones took a different approach using a '55 front on his '57 convertible custom that also uses a Corvette grille insert and chopped top for a striking effect.

BELOW: Another custom convertible, this time Connie and Marlyn Ehglert's full custom '56 model that they bought new and started customising right way. It's been through several phases, was sold, then bought back and refined even more.

BELOW RIGHT: There was even a section for model Chevys including Douglas Faulds' smart '56 210 sedan towing its stock car themed '55 version on a trailer.

BOTTOM: Taking pride of place outside the door to the Convention Centre was the clean '56 two door wagon of Brent and Lori Clark with unusual triple tone paint scheme and billet five spoke wheels. The custom Chevys were on display inside the Convention Centre Ballroom.

LEFT & BELOW: Why not turn your '57 Chevy into a custom hot rod? Dave Hopson completed the nifty hot rod using all metal panels and powered it with a 350 small block V8 engine backed with a Super T10 transmission and '63 Jag rear end. Topping the engine is a rare four carb equipped Man-a-Fre intake manifold.

RIGHT: Jacked up gasser style 210 sedans like this nicely finished '55 with blown small block V8 engine were very popular at the Tri-Five Nationals.
BELOW: Yes, it is a genuine '55 Pace Car as used at Indianapolis on May 30, 1955 and still in all original condition.

ABOVE: Patina encrusted pickup has period perfect bicycle in the bed and a blown 572 Chevy big block up front!
LEFT: How a '55 Suburban panel truck might have looked – if the factory had made one! Dave and Andrea Lukinuk made this one up to look like a factory prototype, but it's all from Dave's own fertile imagination and beautifully executed.

BELOW: Classic Chevys like Robert McCarry's '57 Sports Coupe respond well to complimentary two-tone colour schemes, especially when carried through to interior and wheels.
BOTTOM LEFT: More classic models, this time a garage diorama by Ayden Massey.

ABOVE: Fiano Guzzo brought along his '57 210 sedan based Gasser "The All American" that features fuel injection and fenderwell headers.
BELOW: Randy and Cheri Nelson own "The Rebel Rouser" a '55 210 gasser with blown small block V8, fenderwell headers and ten spoke front wheels. Love the candy striped roof, a common touch on gassers of the sixties.

ABOVE & LEFT: And now a golden gasser, the fabulously detailed '55 210 sedan of Ray Thenot with tunnel ram equipped big block Chevy engine, fenderwell headers, straight axle front end and chromed Cragar S/S wheels. Perfect!

BELOW: Look twice, it's not a Nomad but a '57 sedan delivery with Nomad tailgate strips and appropriate Tennessee licence plate that reads "MAD DLV".

LEFT: One more '56 gasser, this time a two-tone grey and maroon Sports Coupe owned by Lee Jo Sanchez with bible quotation across the trunk. Slow cruising through the car park show and shine area was a popular choice.

ALAN J SMITH (THE KNIGHT OF THE BRUSH)

Where do I start, I began a five year apprenticeship in 1961, it was for signwriting/screen printing, after that I trained in calligraphy and commercial art and I worked for various companies around Sydney where I grew up. I lived in the southern suburbs, the Shire as it is known. I started work in the early '70s as a signwriter at a sign company, Graphic Displays where, over a 12 month period, I progressed to MD, moved the shop to Leichhardt where I turned it into one of the biggest sign shops in the country employing around 20 people and turning over $100,000.00 a month. From there I started Australian Fastsigns that ran extremely well. Meantime I went through a couple of marriages due to the many hours I had to put in. Around 2000 I went solo as I am now doing and enjoying, I have been playing with hot rods since I was 14 and I still do, having nearly completed a Model A roadster. I love the show scene where I demonstrate my trade as a pinstriper which I have been doing all my life. I am now 72 years of age.

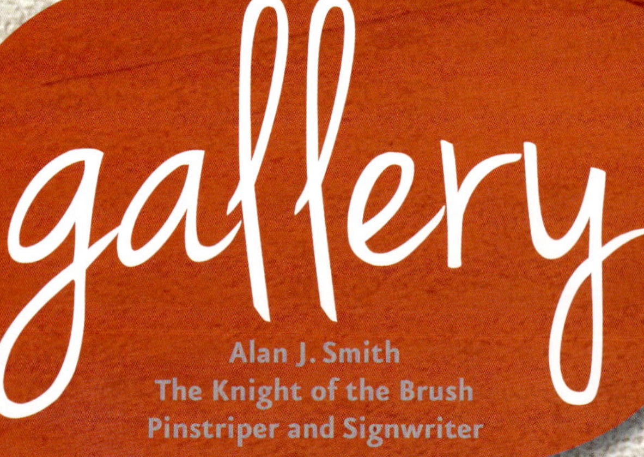

gallery

Alan J. Smith
The Knight of the Brush
Pinstriper and Signwriter

ABOVE: Alan's '27 original T roadster pickup hot rod that acted as a rolling billboard for his talents as a pinstriper and flame painter. The Model T was small block Ford powered and featured red interior trim.

RIGHT: Alan adds some striping to a Morris Minor convertible that was auctioned at the 2019 Sydney Hot Rod and Custom Auto Expo with the proceeds going to charity. One of Alan's popular Rat Fink style trash cans and a sample of his striping from the trunk of a custom car.

Alan Smith
CHP·58V

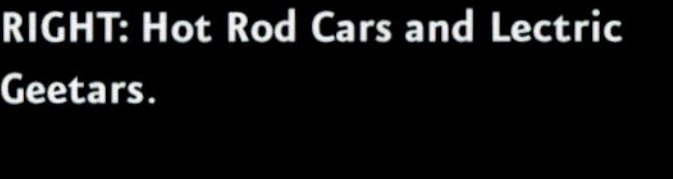

ABOVE: Blue and white striping on a metal seat divider.

ABOVE RIGHT: Graphic sign from Alan Smith's own work van.

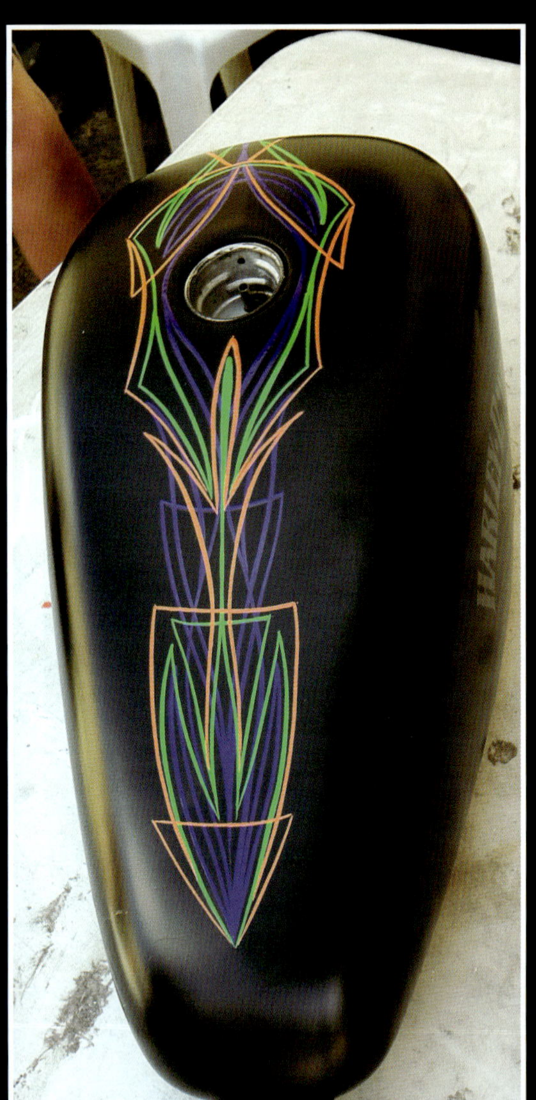

RIGHT: Hot Rod Cars and Lectric Geetars.

LEFT: Multi colour stripes on a motorcycle fuel tank.

BELOW: Chrysler Royal was easily identified as Alan's own car by the wild set of flames.

BOTTOM: White pattern striping on a pickup tailgate.

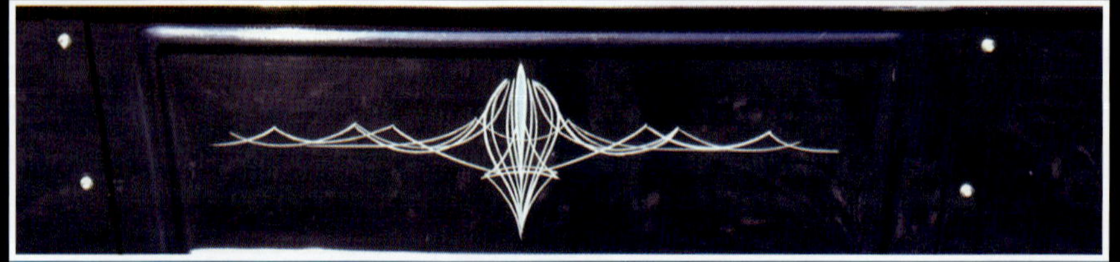

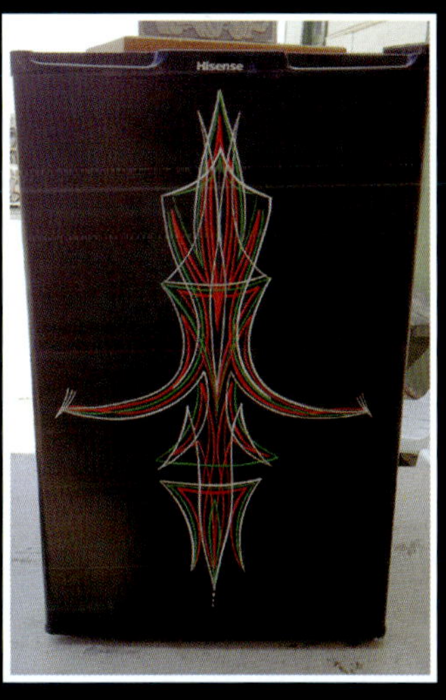

TOP LEFT: Lettering was all hand done on Bill Warner's Super Modified speedway racer.

TOP RIGHT: Rat Fink and flames on fridges.

ABOVE LEFT & CENTRE: Red, green and white striping on satin black.

ABOVE RIGHT: Louvres highlighted with red and white striping.

BELOW LEFT: T Ford coupe has white scallops outlined in red splashed over grille shell and cowl on a T coupe.

BELOW RIGHT: Alan's cartoon character trash cans are popular items at hot rod shows around Sydney, Australia.

ABOVE: Green and lilac stripes on a bowling pin.

ABOVE: Signed panel on the side of a bar fridge.

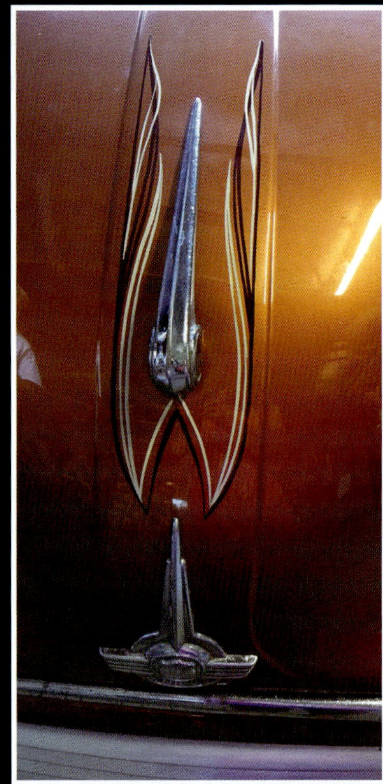

ABOVE RIGHT: Highlight pinstriping to accentuate the bonnet emblem on a Morris custom car.

LEFT & BELOW LEFT: Romans Hot Rod Association barbecue trailer.

BELOW: Hollywood at Home van with elaborate signs on both sides completed by Alan Smith. It was all done on vinyl before wraps were invented, hand painted, cut out and stuck on as he wanted to be able to remove the vinyl when he sold the van.

FAR LEFT & LEFT: Skateboard designs and a beautiful gold striped motorcycle tank.

BELOW: Left-handed Alan working on the end and sides of an old ice chest design.

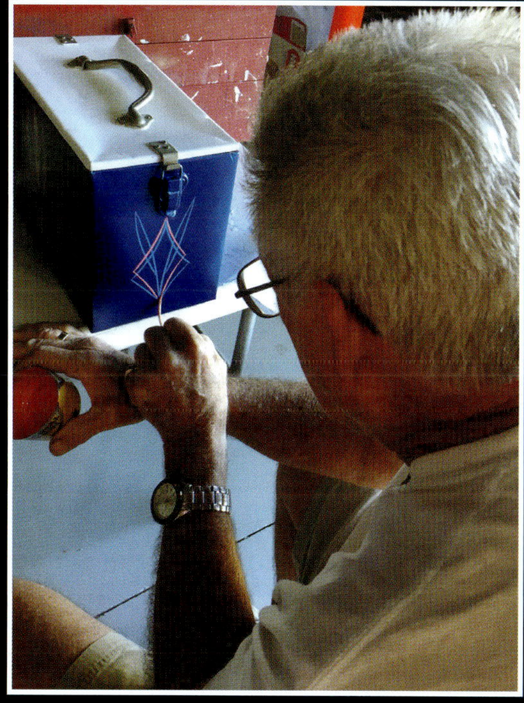

ABOVE: More typical Alan Smith flames, this time on a '32 Ford hiboy roadster Alan hand built with Nick Rees, then took moulds from this car and made his own version.

RIGHT: Green and white striping on a German style helmet.

BELOW RIGHT: Rat Fink and Betty Boob trash cans are popular at hot rod shows.

BELOW LEFT: Yes, guitars get the Smith treatment too!

RIGHT: Even luggage gets the pinstriping treatment.

ABOVE: Alan has built himself a new, more refined version of his roadster shown on the intro page of this article. Note the differences - beige trim, chrome wheels instead of caps and no master cylinder hanging off the firewall.

ABOVE RIGHT CENTRE: Mail boxes get the touch – flames and striping.

ABOVE RIGHT: Years of experience mean Alan can even pinstripe in hard to access chopped hot rods like this Model A coupe.

RIGHT: Another trunk motif on a custom car.

BELOW: Red over beige paintwork really brings this hot rod to life.

BELOW CENTRE: Advertising for Sailor Jerry's on a skateboard platform.

BELOW RIGHT: Rat Fink on a small caravan makes it unique.

ABOVE: Lettering on drag racer, Warren Armour's chopped FJ Holden sedan.

ABOVE RIGHT: Aqua and white motif on the rear of a roadster.

RIGHT: A large expanse of glossy painted sheet metal is highlighted with pink and purple striping.

BELOW: Alan at full concentration while working on a Deuce roadster.

ABOVE: The spare wheel cover on a custom car continental kit is brought to life with a pinstriped motif by Alan Smith.

GRAND NATIONAL ROADSTER SHOW

**Words &
Photos:
Greg Stokes**

2019

As Good As It Gets . . . The 70th Grand National Roadster Show, Pomona, California, USA

The world's longest running indoor show celebrated its 70th birthday over the last weekend of January 2019 in Pomona, California, USA. The Grand National Roadster Show (GNRS) didn't just turn 70, it also enjoyed a very high attendance due to the diverse quality the show offers. Considered to be the greatest indoor hot rod and custom car show on earth, the GNRS attracts visitors from all over the world. If you have never attended, the GNRS is really a must-do on any hot rod or custom car enthusiast's bucket list.

Founded by Al and Mary Slonaker and originally called the Oakland Roadster Show in Northern California, it was John Buck who took over ownership in 2004 moving the three day event south to Pomona, California. A truly time proven prestigious event, this year boasted 500 display vehicles over seven buildings plus another 500 visiting outdoor display cars as part of the Saturday and Sunday drive in.

ABOVE: Troy Trepanier built the Blowfish Barracuda for George Poteet several years ago and it is a regular competitor at Bonneville where it turns speeds in the 300 MPH region.

ABOVE LEFT: Channelled and fendered '32 Ford roadster is an individual style that stands out from the crowd. It's a restored old rod from Texas and was shown under the name "Tweety" and was a AMBR contender.

MAIN PIC: "Building 9" hosted the GNRS tribute to the 90th Anniversary of the Model A, highlighted by this display of all the AMBR winning Model As. At front left is Bill Niekamp's blue roadster that won the very first AMBR title, beside it is the red semi custom Model A roadster of Jerry Woodward who won the AMBR big prize in 1957.

Of course the America's Most Beautiful Roadster Award was a main attraction, as was the Suede Palace and in Building 9, the 90th Anniversary of the Model A Ford.

This year at the 70th GNRS there was a New Zealand element with yours truly being asked to join the judging panel for America's Most Beautiful Roadster (AMBR). "At first I thought someone was pranking me, but it was too good an opportunity to turn down. The AMBR award has been contested

ABOVE: Until you get up close to one of these Lincoln coupes, it is hard to imagine how big they are. Built by Roy Brizio Street Rods for Larry and Juana Carter, it has Ford Coyote running gear and loads of style.

LEFT: The 22 JR Model A roadster was a drag strip terror campaigned by Tony Nancy in the 1960s and now owned by Ross Myer.

BELOW: Light green paint, low stance and attention to detail make this early Corvette a real stand out. The full build was done by Steve's Auto Restorations.

BOTTOM: A project car from South City Rod & Custom was this blue '50 Ford woody with late model undercarriage.

since 1950 and there's considerable history attached to the nine feet tall trophy".

This year there were 14 cars contending for the big trophy and each of those cars were finished to an incredible standard. There were nine judges coming from all corners of the hot rod industry and the judging process was intense with much consideration taken regarding design, themes, finish and detail. "Each of the 14 cars were winners in their own right, but it comes down to what makes for a beautiful roadster in terms of design and style and fit and finish". George Poteet's 1936 Ford roadster built by Pinkee's Rod Shop in Colorado became a clear winner.

Despite what the event title says, the Grand National Roadster Show is a whole lot more than just roadsters. Spanning over six buildings of the Pomona Fairplex, the GNRS features all types of hot rods, customs, low riders, custom VWs, muscle cars, street machines and race cars. For the 2020 event and into the future, ARP Fasteners have come on board to raise the profile of the AMBR award and also the Al Slonaker Memorial Award (for non-roadster vehicles). To conclude, the Grand National Roadster show offers something for everyone including live bands, trade vendors, merchandise and some of the world's best hot rods and custom cars all under one roof.

ABOVE: At first glance you might not notice that this tourer is actually a Model T. It has been fitted with a Deuce grille and tilting roof that changes its style dramatically.

ABOVE RIGHT: Those who like something different will warm to this Buick tourer with twin carb equipped straight eight engine.

RIGHT: You can tell Vern Hammond's yellow Model A roadster is a survivor from another era with its multi-carbed Olds engine, cycle fenders and laid back windshield posts. It was built in 1958-59 by Kim Blackwell and featured on the cover of Hot Rod Magazine.

RIGHT: Deep candy cherry Model A roadster looks just about perfect sitting up on its show stands with all original Model A appointments intact.

BELOW: This was the first time the Ala Kart and the Emperor had been parked side by side since 1960. Barris built the Ala Kart for Richard Peters and the Emperor for Chuck Krikorian. The Ala Kart won in 1958 and 1959 while the Emperor took the big prize in 1960.

TOP & ABOVE LEFT INSET: Two famous hot rods from long ago are the violet Model A roadster of Rich Guasco that won the AMBR in 1961 and he still owns it to this day. The tilt up '30 A roadster was built by Russ Meeks using an Olds Toronado transaxle mounted in the rear. Current owners are Roman and Judy Baszniak.

ABOVE LEFT: Old timey Model A hiboy has a racing history but these days sees regular street duty by owner Brian Bauer who was one of the prime movers behind the 90th Anniversary Model A feature of the GNRS. The roadster is four cylinder Chevy powered.

ABOVE: Tidy '32 Ford pickup is a Street Rodder Road Tour project car with a new United Pacific body.

LEFT: Bright yellow track-nosed Model A roadster was one of Goodguy Gary Meador's own hot rods that he used regularly. The white Model A Sport Coupe was a Rod & Custom Magazine cover car of the early '90s.

TOP: The Suede Palace is where the retro style rods and customs like this Chevy and Model A Coupe are displayed.

TOP RIGHT: Swoopy Caddy coupe just oozes appeal thanks to Foose design.

ABOVE: There's a S.C.o.T. blown Ardun powering Amie and Teri Angelo's '36 Ford three window coupe that was built by Roseville Rod & Custom.

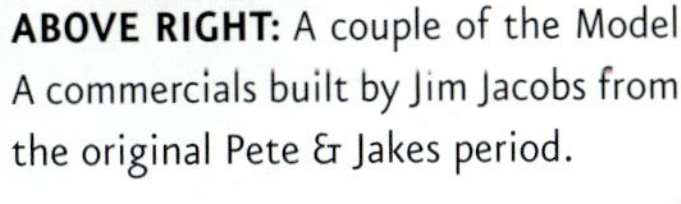

ABOVE RIGHT: A couple of the Model A commercials built by Jim Jacobs from the original Pete & Jakes period.

ABOVE: The nifty Offy powered Model A roadster pickup was built by the late Bob Anderson, while the extended cab Model A pickup was built by PC3g for Chuck DeHeras.

ABOVE: Lots of individual styling details incorporated into this radically chopped '30 Model A Ford coupe with blown Ardun engine.

LEFT: Chad Adams from Adams Hot Rod Shop in Georgia had his superb dark blue '32 Ford roadster in the running for the 2019 AMBR trophy.

BELOW: Everyone remembers Jim Jacobs' decoupage Model A Tourer with Deuce shell. Jake surprised everyone by painting it with a brush at an early Goodguys event and then returning the next year to add all the magazine pages.

BOTTOM: Only one car can win the America's Most Beautiful Roadster trophy and this time it was George Poteet's '36 Ford roadtser built by Pinkee's Rod Shop from Colorado. The superb roadster has been subtly refined and modified from end to end, but still looks like a '36 Ford.

RIGHT: Three different styles of street rods in the outdoor display area. Left to right we have '32 Ford three window coupe, '32 Ford roadster and '37 Ford Business Coupe and all built by Ryan Reed.

BELOW: Don Lindfors drives his '32 Ford roadster pickup all over California these days but it was a former AMBR contender. Powering the pickup is a Boss 302 Ford engine.

RIGHT: Yes, it's an Edsel, but not like any other Edsel you have seen. The stylish red and white two door was built by Bobby Alloway.

BELOW: How radical do you want your Pontiac pickup? This one with fuel trailer in tow was displayed in the outdoor display area.

BELOW RIGHT: Ross Myer's black and blue '32 Ford tourer is a product of the Roy Brizio shop. It uses a brand new reproduction steel two door body designed by Chip Foose and manufactured by Brookville Roadster.

ABOVE: Just let your eyes rest awhile on Rick Dore's coachbuilt aluminium '37 roadster that flows perfectly from end to end.

TOP RIGHT: Check out the swoopy styling of this Deuce phaeton that uses a new Brookville steel two door body and six Stromberg 97s on a Hemi engine.

ABOVE: Paint schemes don't come much wilder than this multi-hued example on a '64 Chevy hardtop.

ABOVE RIGHT: Steve Moal built this scaled-down '32 roadster in collaboration with Jackie Howerton who has a speedway background that is reflected in the styling of the car.

ABOVE: This '33 Ford roadster was built 20 years ago but revamped by Dominator Street Rods for the 2019 AMBR competition.

ABOVE RIGHT: Bill Ganahl of South City Rods & Customs was inducted into the GNRS Hall of Fame for his contiribution to hot rodding. This '34 Coupe is typical of the work from Bill's shop and he had a hand in the restoration of such show winners as the Ala Cart, Sam Barris Merc, Jack Calori's '36 Ford coupe and the Tom McMullen '32 roadster.

RIGHT: Old style lakes roadsters are the black Model A of Billy Crewl with sweeping side pipes and the black and orange version that is obviously GMC powered.

ABOVE: That's a blown big block Chevy in the engine bay of this stylish black cherry '34 Ford phaeton.

LEFT: Manuel Reyes painted those famous flames that appeared on Pete Chapouris' California Kid '34 Ford coupe years ago, but this is his own '36 Ford three window coupe that he built over an extended period.

RIGHT: Four banger power in a '30 Model A Ford is still a popular choice, especially with an overhead valve conversion, finned side plate and a pair of Stromberg 97 carbies like on this example.

ABOVE: Injected Ardun power is just right for this brown Model A hiboy roadster on '32 rails. Cowl mounted steering and early Ford wire wheels just add to the aura of a nicely balanced rod that was built by Hilton Hot Rods.

Our correspondent, Greg Stokes was invited to take part in the judging of America's Most Beautiful Roadster for 2019, an honour and an opportunity he couldn't knock back. Nine judges combine their opinions and expertise to find the overall winner. Greg says the calibre of the judges brings a balance of neutral and non-emotional judging and it's a brutal and unforgiving and as passionate as you might imagine, but it is a fair process and they are judging America's Modst Beautiful Roadster, not the most traditional or the most driven.

The judging process starts on the Wednesday before the show when the contenders are driven into the hall and right up to the judge's table. This is an important aspect of the judging process as they can admire (or not) the car as it comes toward them and see how it looks and sounds from all angles. They can also determine how comfortable the driver is in the car and how they control its movements. It is interesting to note that a couple of the contenders failed on this point straight away.

Once parked, the owner then has a 10-15 minute window to talk with the judges, describe the theme and build process of the car and highlight anything the judges might miss. A few of the owners handed out "build books" that really showcased the extent of the work put into the particular car. By the end of the day it was clear there were three top cars amongst the 14 contenders.

The cars are then set up in their displays and the judges have from opening time on Friday at noon until Saturday night to further inspect the 14 cars before meeting together and going around the table to select the overall winner.

The award isn't about the biggest spender wins – it's about styling, theme, fit and finish, design and fabrication and the way the whole package is presented.

Sting in

Pete Jackson, 1932 Ford Three Window Coupe, Norfolk UK

the Tail

There's nothing quite like a full-on hot rod to evoke everything that we like to think of as raw performance. Bright orange paint, a 461 cubic inch engine and a quarter mile time slip at Santa Pod raceway of 9.981@132 mph wrapped up in a package of '32 Ford three window coupe fits that raw performance hot rod description to perfection. Here's how it came about for English hot rodder and drag racer, Pete Jackson.

Pete started out with a pair of American Stamping chassis rails that he boxed, outfitted with a chrome moly tube X member, Model A front crossmember, chrome moly spreader bar and removed the rear frame horns. Over that he dropped a Rodline fibreglass body that he purchased back in 1998 with a 3-1/2 inch roof chop, opening screen and a recessed firewall. This dual purpose street rod was always going drag racing, so a 10 point 4130 chrome moly roll cage was built into the body as well.

Underpinning the coupe is suspension that consists of a Magnum four inch dropped tube axle held in place by a chrome moly four bar with owner fabricated bat-wings, brackets and bracing. Custom alloy front hubs carry Wilwood disc brakes with four piston calipers, while a Mustang steering box mounted in right hand drive cross steer configuration connects to a Mustang tilt column topped by a Grant steering wheel.

Waiting to absorb the enormous output from the engine/trans combination is a Ford nine inch rear end that has been narrowed, fitted with 4.11 gears, Strange Pro race shafts and custom made brackets and bracing. Holding it in place is another chrome moly Pro Mod specification four link system with diagonal locater all fabricated by Chris Isaacs Race Cars and a custom made drive shaft with heavy duty universal joints. Suspension is by Avo coil-overs and stock Ford drum brakes are retained at each end of the housing.

All that heavy duty equipment is in there to absorb the torque from the Bill Michael Hard Core Racing Products (World Products) and is based on a 461 cubic inch "Man-o-War" small block Ford engine that runs 10.5:1 compression, a full roller cam and World Senior heads fed by a Dominator carburettor. That's all as per spec as a crate engine that puts out 635bhp@6000 rpm and 615 ft lb torque@4800 rpm. In that "stock" form the car ran 10.8@121 mph but since then the compression has been revised, along with the fuel system, jetting and ignition. The result was 9.98@132 mph – impressive! Sanderson Sprint headers with 3-1/2 inch collectors and header caps feed the exhaust into 3-1/2 inch pipes under the chassis with Borla ZR1 mufflers. The radiator is a custom made aluminium version made shorter to allow clear air to get to the intake scoop sitting behind the fibreglass grille shell that is fitted with a Vintique stainless steel insert. A 16 inch electric fan and electric water pump make it all work effectively.

So much torque needs a transmission that can take the brute torque as well, so a TCI C6 manual body reverse shift pattern race box was fitted with a TCI 10 inch 4800 rpm stall speed converter, SFI flex plate and flex plate shield, plus a B&M Pro Ratchet shifter and a stand alone transmission cooler.

Okay, there's no doubt Pete achieved his aims when it comes to producing horsepower and torque but you have to plant it on the road surface too. How about a pair of 12x15 ET Fueler rear rims with 315/60/15 Mickey Thompson street radial pro tyres and skinny 4x15 ET 12 spoke bolt-on front rims with Firestone F560 tyres.

In the trunk is an alloy nine gallon fuel tank that feeds the monster heavy doses of Sunoco race fuel via a Pro Star 500 fuel pump and filter through braided stainless steel lines. The Optima battery also lives in the trunk.

Now back to that Chris Boyle made fibreglass body. It has been fitted with an opening windscreen using 6mm laminated glass, single skin doors with Lexan side and rear windows, a removable, louvered

WARNING
THE DRIVER OF THIS VEHICLE
IS NOT AUTHORISED TO CARRY
PASSENGERS. ANY PERSONS
WHO ACCEPT A LIFT DO SO
COMPLETELY AT THEIR OWN RISK.

steel trunk lid that is bonded into the fibreglass frame, rolled rear pan, '48 Ford taillights and a Deist parachute. And the paint colour – just orange, vivid, hit-you-in-the-face orange!

Last thing to do is check out the interior. Nestled inside that 10 point roll cage is a pair of Jazz bucket seats, five point racing harness, a B&M Pro Ratchet shifter and buttons for Line Locker and trans brake. Moon and Auto Meter gauges keep Pete informed when his foot is down and there's a kill switch and fire extinguisher in case things go wrong. Other switches are housed in an overhead panel and a Lokar parking brake stops the coupe from rolling away when parked.

Pete's coupe is legally road registered in the UK and races in the Outlaw Class at Santa Pod Raceway.

NGK
SPARK PLUGS
NGK
SPAR
M 96.2 RADIO

ABOVE: A stop-off at the Case family in Toowoomba before heading to the first night's stop at Miles. Malcolm's green '32 Tudor is at the rear and son, Josh's new Model A roadster is in front. The orange '32 Ford Tudor is run host, Greg Thomsen's own car.
MAIN PIC: The painted silos at Thallon provide a startling backdrop for the group of run participants on the fourth day of Greg's 7 day run.

Words & Photos: Greg Thomsen and others

Greg's 7 Day Run

Wandering around Queensland and New South Wales in Street Rods makes for a fun vacation

Greg's Seven Day Run was a low-key adventure into outback Queensland and NSW by a small group of street rodders in February 2019. Organised by Greg Thomsen, the run attracted nine entries that set off on their adventure immediately after the High Altitude Rod Run at Toowoomba.

The group covered 1600 kilometres on the trip with all participants voting it a great success. The first night stop-over was at Miles, just three hours from Toowoomba. The second day was also a leisurely day of only four hours driving that took in the townships of Glenmorgan and Surat, ending at St George for the overnight stay. After stops at Nindigully, Thallon and Mungindi, the group crossed into NSW on the third day, with Moree being the destination for the overnight stop. From there it was only a short drive to Inverell on the fourth day and on to Glen Innes on the fifth day, enroute to Tenterfield. Another short journey on the sixth day ended at Casino before all returned home to the Brisbane area on day seven. Photos accompanying this article were supplied by various members of the group and clearly indicate a good time was had by all as they tripped around, taking in the sights and visiting various rodders and car enthusiasts along the way.

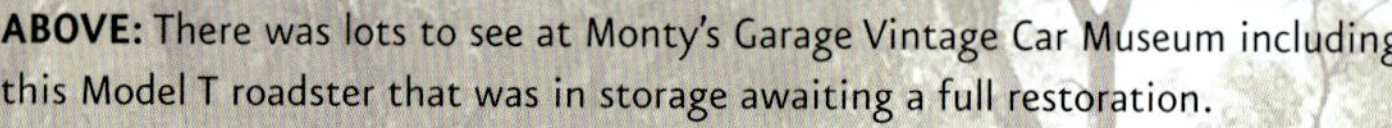

ABOVE: There was lots to see at Monty's Garage Vintage Car Museum including this Model T roadster that was in storage awaiting a full restoration.

ABOVE: Flathead engine was part of the display at Monty's Garage.
MAIN PIC: You know you're in the country! The cattle were easy to pass – but the next 10 kilometres were spent dodging cow pats!

ABOVE LEFT: Dubbed as "The Grey Ghost II", this Redex branded '48 Ford sedan is one of the display cars at Monty's Garage, Glenmorgan.

ABOVE RIGHT: Peter and Janelle Tight wait for service for their two door Chrysler Newport at Monty's Garage.

LEFT: More from the collection at Monty's Garage at Glenmorgan. The car appears to be about '29 or '30 Reo Flying Cloud.

ABOVE: Event organiser, Greg Thomsen makes a "fuel stop" at Monty's Garage on the second day of the 7 Day Rod Run.

ABOVE: More of the collection at Monty's, this time some restoration projects waiting their turn. The Ford single spinner ute looks to be quite complete.

ABOVE: The second night was in St George so a trip to the winery was the first stop before moving on to Nindigully.

ABOVE & LEFT: Got to the famous Nindigully Pub just in time to have a beer at 10:00am – yep, just one! It's in the middle of nowhere, but tourist buses and caravans were calling in. The pub features in an Aussie beer commercial on television.

LEFT: The National Transport Museum at Inverell had a great variety of exhibits. Most of the display cars in this picture are vintage era to late 1940s.

BELOW LEFT: Hamming it up in the National Transport Museum.

BELOW: Nothing like a drive in the country in your street rod.

ABOVE: What's a rod run without a breakdown? This was just out of Moree NSW. Greg's Tudor lost drive, turned out to be an easy fix, just a new governor gear.
BELOW: The National Transport Museum at Inverell had lots to see including this Model A tourer street rod and XY GT Falcon.

ABOVE: Rod and Faye Axelsen's fuel injected Holden powered '36 Ford coupe has covered 160,000 kilometres in 14 years, including two trips across the Nullabor.
BELOW: Figuring out a credit card only fuel up in Surat – Leon Birss in the T coupe and Glenn Czislowski in the Chevy pickup.

BELOW: Ken and Marie Mitchell knocked the bottom out of the oil pan on a cattle grid. The Townsend family in Glen Innes came to the rescue and repaired it.

ABOVE: Another one of the Townsend projects at Glen Innes was this currently all original '35 Ford Tudor.

BELOW LEFT: The participants; Greg and Anita Thomsen, Al and Di Neary, Ken and Marie Mitchell, Carol and Gordon Bruback, Glenn and Moyra Czislowski, David and Lynne Fairbrother, Faye and Rod Axelsen, Leon Birss and missing were Peter and Jannelle Tight.

BELOW RIGHT: Participants gather around the table for a group photo at dinner time on the last night in Casino.

ABOVE: Gordon and Carol Bruback came along for this trip in their rare "aerodynamic" '34 Hupmobile.
ABOVE RIGHT: Rod and Faye Axelesen in the '36 Ford coupe, Al and Di Neary in the '33 Ford coupe (with '34 hood).
RIGHT: Some flathead Ford eye candy in Glen Innes.
BELOW: It was a hot 41°C at Thallon, hence the conveyor being used for shade while photographing the painted silos that appear in the intro photo.

BELOW LEFT: John Townsend's big block Chevy powered '32 Ford roadster.
BELOW: John Townsend's small block Chevy powered '32 Ford sedan.

NSRA Nationals

LOUISVILLE, KENTUCKY

The 50th Anniversary was a knockout!

Words & Photos: Larry O'Toole & Al O'Toole

The 50th Anniversary NSRA Street Rod Nationals was always destined to be a big affair. Just how big was anyone's guess, but it soon became apparent once registrations opened on the day before the official start of the Nationals. By mid-morning the line of late entrants waiting to be processed extended the full length of the Cardinals Stadium registration room, in addition to four or five lines across the room at the registration tables. Never had I seen this many people at registration at the one time in the past – and it kept up at that rate all day long. Pre-entrants were smart, they were able to walk right up and collect their credentials with minimum waiting.

Our 42 strong NSRA Tour group bargained on getting through the registration process in about 30 minutes, giving us time to have a quick lunch nearby and then head for our tour of the Jim Beam distillery. That plan soon changed as it took over an hour just to wait in line, so the lunch stop was cancelled and once registration was completed we headed straight for the Jim Beam stop, half an hour drive south of Louisville. Fortunately, their small kiosk was able to supply basic burgers and sandwiches, so nobody went hungry.

Following the Jim Beam visit it was time for some shopping and rest prior to our welcome dinner at Doc Crow's in downtown Louisville on Wednesday evening. Thursday morning the Nationals started in earnest with lines of street rods and customs similar to what would normally be expected on Friday or Saturday. There was a feeling in the air that this was going to be a very big Nationals. Confirmation came as soon as we were in the fairgrounds where more than the usual parking spots occupied on a Friday were already taken up – and this was first thing Thursday morning!

It was more of the same within the swap meet area as much larger than usual crowds milled about the sites looking for a bargain. Inside the massive commercial building it was also very busy, crowds more expected of a Friday or Saturday than the very first few hours of the event.

Friday morning is set up time for the popular Pro's Pick event within the Nationals providing the best opportunity to see many of the top cars in the one place as they jockey for the attention of the selection committee to hopefully make the Top 12 at Sunday's Award Presentations. In recent years the

RIGHT: Tribute display section featured the prominent Pete and Jake's coupes from the 1970s and even included that famous Rod & Custom chicken coupe cover!

ABOVE: What a fine line up of Deuces, all showing off their finest in the Pro's Pick area. Left to right they are: Stan Springs, Charlotte, North Carolina, Bob Cook, Fresno, California and the red one belongs to Bill Collins of Greeneville, Tennessee.

variety of contenders for this Pro's Pick has been very interesting and it was this time too. Everything from high end pro-built cars to basic, but cleverly put together drivers and of all makes and models. No longer is Pro's Pick just the realm of the Ford based cars.

The people and entrant cars just kept rolling in, making Friday more like the busiest of Saturdays, and Saturday almost completely maxed out. Cars were squeezed into every nook and cranny within the fairgrounds, as they had to be, the final count for entries was 12,762! That wasn't an all-time record, but not far short of it and a big increase on the common figure of around 10,000 entries of recent years.

Another noticeable change was inside the commercial building where the trade stands have been spaced out over recent years to fill the gaps. This time they were much more densely packed in and they all did a roaring trade from the constant waves of visitors. It is very hard to know how many people attended the Nationals but my guess would be in excess of 150,000. By the close of the Nationals on Sunday afternoon, some of the commercial booths that were packed full of stock

at the start of the event were all but stripped bare. There are going to be a lot more hot rods hitting the road soon, going by the amount of merchandise purchased at this one event.

There are so many aspects to the Nationals that it is hard to describe them all, and harder still to take them all in. Apart from the highlights I have mentioned here there is Womens World and the Ladies Afternoon Tea, the Streetkhana driving events, the specialist shows like Mopar Country and Under 29, the Builders Showcase presentation in the corridor along the side of the commercial building and of course the never-ending array of street rods, customs and classics on display right throughout the Kentucky Exposition Centre.

Anyone that attended the NSRA 50th Anniversary Street Rod Nationals will have it etched in their memory for a long time. It was a beauty, so glad we got to enjoy the experience with many other Aussies, around 100 of whom were in attendance at our International Reception on the Saturday morning.

BELOW: An early visit to the swap meet at the Nationals is advisable and don't hesitate if you see something you want. More than likely it won't be there if you go back later. There's always a huge variety of rod building material on hand from whole cars to the smallest parts.

ABOVE: An hour or two just inside the main gate soon gives you a perspective of how big the Nationals has grown. Rods keep coming at you four or five abreast like this – non-stop!

ABOVE: The swap meet is a great place to pick up a pickup that is ready for you to complete. This one was advertised at $22,500.00 and had "sold" written across the sticker. The entire rolling chassis was fully updated in typical street rod fashion.

ABOVE RIGHT: The seminar series hosted by SEMA is growing each year. This was a typical crowd for almost all of the seminars this year.

BELOW: Neat as a pin '36 Ford five window coupe of Jim Evans had 312 Y block Ford running gear and cream wheels with whitewall tyres.

ABOVE: The NSRA had two give-away cars for lucky entrants at the 50th Anniversary Nationals. The maroon Chevelle was given away on Saturday and the blue Deuce Roadster on Sunday.

LEFT: The bugs on the grille and the Deuce Days North West sticker (see page 158) on the windshield indicate this Deuce tourer did a lot of miles to get to Louisville, Kentucky for the 50th Nationals. Bet it was worth it though!

ABOVE: Here's a popular new trend, glossy black running gear and highlights together with skinny conventional look radial tyres on a Deuce roadster. This one, entered by Gary Corkell of Middleown, Delaware, was prominent in the Pro's Pick area. That blown engine is a small block Chevy dressed up to look like an Olds Rocket engine.

NSRA *Nationals*

LEFT & BELOW: A stroll through the Builders' Showcase will expose you to such beauties as this Olds Hardtop Fiesta Wagon owned by Bobby and Carolyn Buttram. The two tone long-roof was built by Cimtex Rods and has matching two tone leather interior trim. Who wouldn't like to park this one on their own garage?

LEFT: Wild cross-ram induction on a Mopar engine is perfect for this black '31 Plymouth coupe that's mounted on a Ford Deuce style chassis. Owner Samuel Woods hails from Elyria, Ohio.

ABOVE & LEFT: Roy and Donna Richardson had One Off Rod & Custom put together this Foose Brookville Roadster two door Deuce tub project with multi-carb equipped Hemi powerplant and superb styling from end to end.

LEFT: In conjunction with the NSRA we hosted an International Reception at the Nationals and it was filled with mostly Aussies, plus a few Kiwis and one Canadian. The short get-together was a great way to meet others from around the world, doing the same thing at the 50th NSRA Street Rod Nationals.

LEFT & BELOW: Impressive is the only way to describe Dan Bouchard's '58 F100 pickup that has been extensively customised, yet still looks like an original Ford item. Major changes to hood, grille, front bumper etc. aren't immediately apparent until you look a little closer and compare to an original vehicle. The work was done by Korek Designs.

MAIN PIC: Rooftop photo reveals a sea of colour below. Note the canopies in the background, none are permitted in the foreground area or you wouldn't see any cars from this vantage point.

NSRA *Nationals*

LEFT & BELOW: A highly detailed flathead engine and black painted early Ford wire wheels are features of this outstanding '32 Ford five window coupe owned by Mike Barillaro and built in his own workshop. It was displayed in the Builders' Showcase section.

BELOW: Remember when Hurst shifters were all the rage? This swap meet vendor has most of them now!

BOTTOM: The Cherry Bomb is a gasser style '57 Chevy drag racer that is powered by a mountainous 468 cubic inch blown big block engine. Owners are Jeff and Tracy Spear.

ABOVE & RIGHT: The Street Rodder magazine stand featured many iconic hot rods from the past including Tom McMullen's flamed '32 Ford hiboy roadster, the ZZ Top '33 Ford coupe and Li'l John Buttera's white Model A hiboy roadster. Buttera is generally credited with kicking off the "billet era" in the late 1970s – early 1980s.

ABOVE: Chevy trucks are hot and everything from the mid-fifties to the early '80s is getting the treatment. At top are two examples from the LMC Trucks booth and the orange example was on the Sanderson Headers stand.

MAIN PIC: A view across the Pro's Pick display area reveals a sea of diverse high quality cars that leave you watering at the mouth. In the foreground we have a bright green '55 Chevy Sports Coupe together with a black Model A Tudor and the blue and white '58 Ford wagon of Gary L Uftring.
LEFT: Front and centre on the Painless Wiring stand was this glossy black '32 Ford roadster owned by Rick Harkleroad with tri-power small block Chevy engine.

LEFT: Fresh out of the Adams Hot Rod Shop was this '33 Ford coupe owned by Chris and Charis Trombetta and featured in the Builders' Showcase section.
BELOW: Another high quality build in the Builders' Showcase section was the light beige '37 Ford Business Coupe of Jim Bridgewater, built by All Ways Hot Rods.
BELOW LEFT: Carl Casper's "Empress" was just one of many show customs that he built back in the day. It's based on a '51 Chevy two door sedan.

LEFT: Nice clean '55 Chevy has a surprise under the hood. Nothing less than a fully Arias Equipped big block Chevy engine that uses every inch of available space. Owner is Brian Baker of Iron City, Ohio.

BELOW: Jacked up, gasser style Model A coupe spent a lot of time cruising the grounds with plenty of advance warning thanks to open headers. Mal and Steve drive it often — just for fun.

ABOVE: Model A Tudors don't come more radical than this one owned by Keith Diehl of Nitro West Virginia, or as well finished. The outstanding, low riding Tudor is blown LS Chevy powered and full of tricks.

ABOVE: Four Aussie cars made it all the way around to the other side of the planet to take part in the Nationals. The green Vauxhall Wyvern Caleche tourer belongs to John and Marie Revill from Western Australia who were delighted to take home the Longest Distance Award. Dean Vanutinni entered his flamed '33 Ford three window coupe that was the Top Steet Rod at the first Goulburn Nationals back home in Australia. Others to make the long trek were Graeme Williams with his T Bucket and Dave Murphy with his '32 Ford hiboy roadster.

LEFT & BELOW: Ponder on this delightful Model A coupe for a while; 331 Hemi engine, teardrop headlights, custom wheel caps, three inch chopped top, whitewalls and details like a one inch channel over the chassis, combined '36 Packard and '37 Ford headlights and a narrowed Buick dash; need I go on? Okay, Deuce chassis, Borg Warner T5 transmission and Winters quick-change rear end. Lucky owner is David Luebcke from Crown Point, Indiana.

ABOVE & RIGHT: Not a model you see every day is the '53 Nash Rambler. This one has been updated a little from stock and is the pride and joy of owner Dennis Quin from Washington, Illinois. In the engine bay is a detailed and stack injected LS1 Chevy V8 engine, the wheels are Billet Specialties and the inside is bathed in red leather trim.

ABOVE: Early woodies like this '36 Ford look fantastic when given the full street rod treatment without compromising the original woodie style. Drew Hopay got it right thanks to Gis Automotive who built the wagon.

RIGHT: Take a tidy '54 Chevy coupe and drop in a W head 409 engine and dress it like this one featured on the ARP Automotive Racing Products stand and you have a real treasure.

ABOVE: Endless line ups of rods and customs like that shown here are everywhere you look in the Kentucky Expo Center while the Nationals is taking place. The '60s style Deuce five window coupe in the foreground is owned by John Bauer – lucky guy!

ABOVE: Willys coupes are as popular as ever, usually done in Gasser style with a big V8 engine. This one owned by Quint Walbverts fits the mould perfectly.
ABOVE RIGHT: Vivid orange '38 Ford Standard coupe of Cornell Woosley demonstrates perfect stance and low profile.

ABOVE: The "Student Grade A" Model A Tudor was built by trainees at the Washtenaw Community College. Looks like we have some talented rod builders coming through.

RIGHT: George Poteet's '36 Ford roadster was an AMBR winner and took its place in the Builder' Showcase section at the Nationals.

MAIN PIC: Roof top view of hundreds of rods and customs pouring through the entry gate is enough to make your heart skip a beat. By close of registrations on Saturday there were 12,762 entries recorded.

ABOVE: Shadow Rods now have a roadster pickup version of their T roadster and it looks rather tasty when given treatment like this version. The owner could have been you as they had this pickup for sale.

LEFT: Deuce woody is a superbly detailed version owned by Orville Adair and was on display in the Pro's Pick area on Friday. Injected small block Chevy provides the motivation, brown leather provides the comfort and the wheels are polished Real Wheels.

TOP LEFT: Who doesn't love a bubble top '61 Chevy with a dressed up 409 and off-white leather interior? Ken Nester parks it in his garage each night.

ABOVE: You won't find a factory one of these anywhere. Woody Smith converted his '38 Ford Deluxe to a three window coupe and slotted a nicely detailed Lincoln V12 in the engine bay.

LEFT: Bernadine Goodwin/Thompson owns this Chevy ute that lives in the USA now. It was originally blue and built by Rod Cahill in Queensland.

BELOW: Different treatment of Derrel and Kane Pesko's '28 Model A Ford Tudor has resulted in an outstanding street rod. There's nothing on this car that doesn't need to be there and its simple clean styling makes it a real stand out. Check out the "deck chair" style interior seating, the art deco dash insert, the smooth, full disc alloy wheels and the low mounting points for the headlights.

ABOVE: Karl Wooldridge's stylish '37 Packard convertible has a surprise under the hood in the form of a "Packardised" Viper V10 engine.

ABOVE RIGHT: Another Packard convertible but this one has the "Packard" treatment on a supercharged Chevy LS engine so it looks like it belongs in there. Owner is Ronald Frederic.

ABOVE: Chad Adams knows how to build a '32 Ford roadster as attested by his blue Y block powered version that was selected in the Top 12 from Pro's Pick. All the work is done in his Calhoun, Georgia workshop.

RIGHT & BELOW: Blacked out '72 Chevy C10 pickup is perfect from end to end and right there with the latest trend to make project cars out of these square look Chevy pickups. Owner of this example is Chuck Moskey.

ABOVE: Nice channelled A roadster sports Hemi powerplant and classic channelled car stance that just makes you want to go for a drive! Blame it on Allen Muttert of Wentzville, Missouri.

ABOVE: Engines; at far left is a flathead conversion to F head design branded Dixon, no doubt very rare. Next is a pair of LS engines with dress up kits to make them look like a big block 396-454 style at the rear, or the desirable W head 348-409 type engine and above is a rebuilt Chrysler D300 383 cubic inch from 1963 complete with cross-ram intake manifold – about as wild as it gets for factory induction.

ABOVE: Flip front '52 Sears Roebuck Allstate (Henry J) has Chrysler Hemi engine and wheelie bars that indicate it goes hard too. Owner, Mark Mahorney brought it to the Nationals from Mt Eden, Kentucky.

ABOVE: A Viper V10 heart lives in the engine bay of Rick and Lynn Talnot's Lincoln Zephyr coupe from Ridgeway, Viriginia.

LEFT: Purple looks good on hot rods and never better than on the '30 Model A coupe of Tom and Jeannie Salinas that features whitewalls and trim rings on white painted wheels. Motive power comes from a Buick Nailhead engine sitting in front of a white firewall and that white theme even extends to the interior trim.

ABOVE: How about a Deuce or two? Make that dozens surrounding this large canopy in the Fairgrounds parking lot where friends gather to enjoy each other's company.

RIGHT: Vivid Gold looks outstanding on Rich and Bev Stapf's Buick Nailhead powered '32 Ford five window coupe.

BELOW RIGHT: All manner of personal transport can be seen at the Nationals but few as original as this fairgrounds bumper car converted to "Gofer" status – with freight trailer!

ABOVE: Yes, some American rods do have cycle guards – like Paul Puleo's highly blinged up, blown big block Chevy powered Deuce coupe.

ABOVE, LEFT & RIGHT: There's always something unusual on the "Absorber" chamois promotional stand in the main building, this time it was Robert Freeman's 215 cubic inch mid "Berlin Buick" engined VW Beetle. Insane!

LEFT: Cruising the fairgrounds is popular so why not take your gasser style '55 Chevies for a spin? In the lead is "Mr Impatient" followed by the Cadillac powered "Mistress".

BELOW: Plenty to see here in Vince Baker's completely hand fabricated aluminium Model A Ford pickup. Gaze awhile and observe the slightly narrowed grille, louvered belly pans, quick-change rear end and matching silver interior trim. Driveline appears to be based on a four cylinder Pinto engine and hidden suspension, quarter elliptic on the rear and torsion bar at the front. Ponder a little longer on all of the custom alloy work in and around the cabin and on things like the door hinges, louvered panels, cowl mounted steering and drilled brackets. There's a lot of individuality here!

ABOVE: Constant long lines of patrons waited at the NSRA merchant booths to buy a souvenir of the Nationals and they sold just about everything they had available.

ABOVE: Stylish is the only way to describe a '47 Mercury convertible finished in bright red with beige interior trim. Harry Hartkemeyer of the Hilltoppers Club brought this one to the 50th Nationals from Cincinnati, Ohio.

ABOVE: Yet another one of those square Chevy pickups that have gained so much in popularity of late. This slammed '70 model is owned by Chris Nunn and runs large diameter plain steel wheels – also suddenly more popular.

ABOVE: How much can you detail a street rod? Ed Sears certainly went the full Monty on his '40 Ford pickup that also has a chopped and lengthened cab, fully dressed 8BA flathead engine under a pie-cut, nosed and sectioned hood and incredible finish everywhere. The "Gold Standard" was a recent Ridler Great Eight finalist and Truck of the Year.

BELOW: Jacked up early '60s Falcon two door sedan looks really cool in vivid red and with 10 spoke wheels up front. These models are popular for such treatment and affordable for younger rodders.

ABOVE One of the original first Nationals participant cars was this Ardun powered T bucket owned and built by Cotton Werksman in the mid-sixties. The bucket is now owned by Gregory Hall and was featured in the 50th Nationals historic display.

LEFT: Another T bucket that Cotton Werksman built in the late sixties with Bob Knack, but this time a flamed flathead powered version also now owned by Gregory Hall. The Ardun flathead engine in the yellow T above originally powered this flamed bucket.

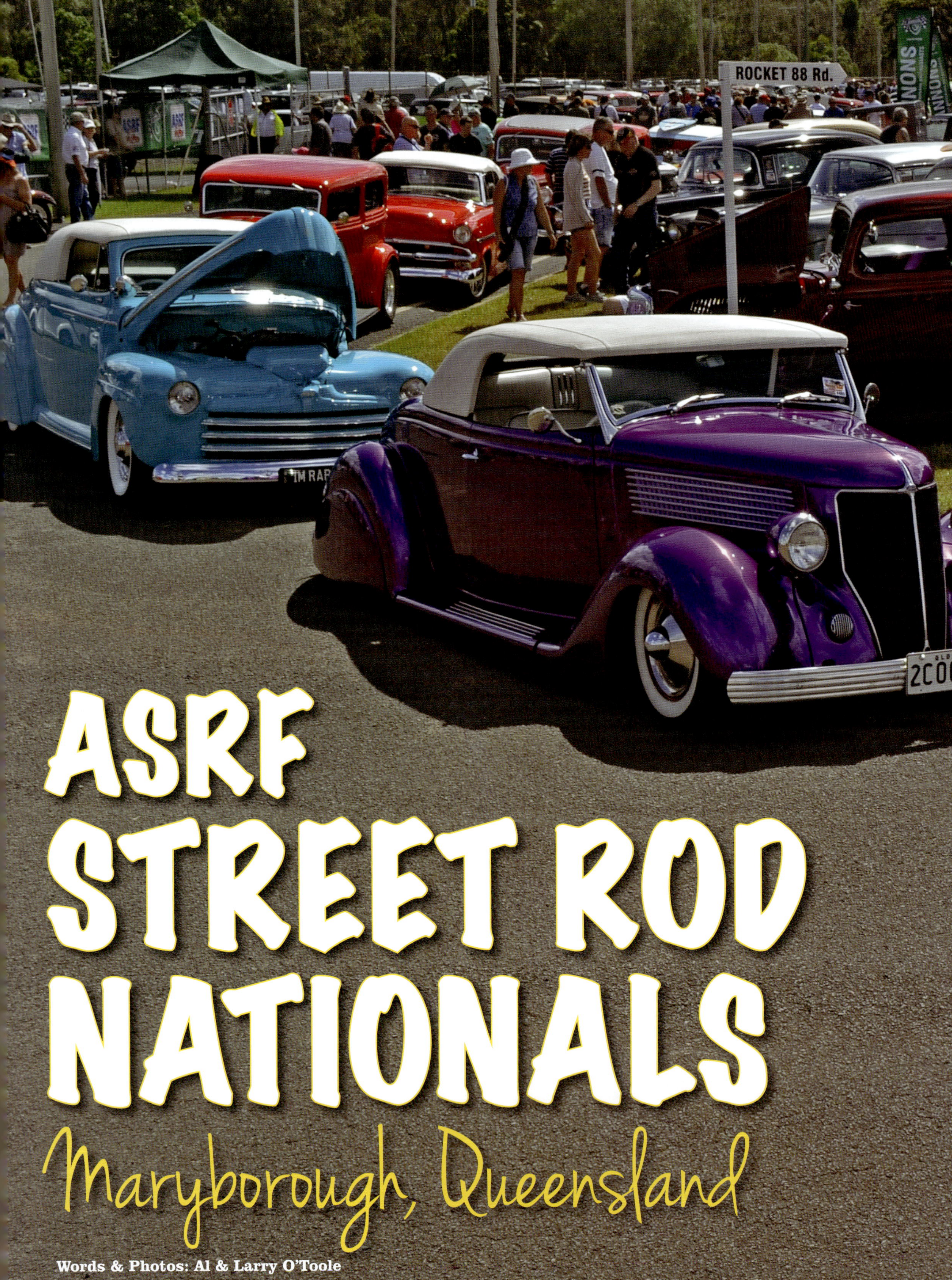

ASRF STREET ROD NATIONALS

Maryborough, Queensland

Words & Photos: Al & Larry O'Toole

The program for the 2019 ASRF Street Rod Nationals provided for an early bump-in period on the Wednesday prior to Easter and early registration from 1:30pm to 4:00pm the same day. Registration continued on Thursday but with the additional attraction of an early-bird cruise to Bundaberg.

Good Friday is always Entrants Only Day at the Aussie Nationals with cruising the grounds, trade stands open and such side events as the Kids Hot Wheels Challenge and Esky racing practise getting under way. In the evening there was a meet and greet in the food hall from 5:00pm and all looked set for a great Nationals.

Then the rain started to fall with greater intensity and it kept up for much of the Friday night. Next morning it was obvious there had been so much rain that the show and shine would not be able to go ahead on the oval infield area of the showgrounds, so a quick executive decision was made to park all of the street rods along the internal sealed roads between the buildings and make the most of an unfortunate situation. Well, that situation turned out to be one of the highlights of the Nationals as everyone enjoyed seeing the cars in that environment even more than they would have if they had been all lined up on the infield. Having the cars displayed like this also brought the people closer to the trade stands and made the whole venue seem more animated. The Nationals was off to a flyer.

From the time the gates opened on Saturday morning there were strong crowd numbers evident and they kept coming. Later reports indicated that over 10,000 people passed through the gates for the day – an outstanding result.

Saturday night the heavens opened up again with consistent heavy rain almost drowning out the entertainment in the huge undercover area. The wet weather meant more of the public parking areas had to be roped off to protect them from further damage as they had become chopped up in places. Fortunately the crowd wasn't quite as large on the Sunday so the facilities coped quite well and once again the street rods were all lined up along the edges of the sealed internal roads.

The main trophies were voted for by entrants' choice and realistically there were probably fifty or more cars that could have scored in the Top 20. When the winners were announced it was obvious that many of them were either built or owned by younger rodders, a good sign that rodding is transitioning to another generation who know what they are doing. Then the big announcement came for Top Car of the Nationals and there was much excitement as Dean Wilson was called up for his outstanding '37 Plymouth coupe. This was the first time in the history of the ASRF Nationals that a non-Ford vehicle has won the big prize and it was greeted with a fantastic round of applause. There is a heart-warming story behind the Wilson coupe winning as well. Dean's father, Errol Wilson started the project but unfortunately passed away several years ago. Dean took over the coupe project and did an outstanding job. It was a very popular win and we featured the car on the cover of ASR issue 349.

After another downpour on Sunday night, the 2019 ASRF Street Rod Nationals wrapped up on the Monday with a cruise to Hervey Bay. The event was a fantastic success and a real boost for the Maryborough community. Now it's time to start planning for the Goulburn Regional Nationals in 2020 and the next major ASRF Street Rod Nationals in Albury 2021.

ABOVE: Down from Rockhampton was Warren Burggraaff in his gunmetal grey 1936 Chevrolet Pickup.

ABOVE: An oldie but a goodie that recently underwent some updating is the '27 T Tudor of Stuart Glover who is a member of Toowoomba Hot Rodders.

RIGHT: Luke Patterson kept his 1938 Dodge Coupe Ute low key with black steel wheels and standard bodywork. Note the coupe body styling line that gave this model a distinctive appearance.

ABOVE: Beware, potent looking '41 Willys coupe on the prowl and this one is owned by drag racer and Gold Coast Street Rodders member, Peter Gratz. That glossy yellow flip front hides a blown Hemi engine that backs up the image in no uncertain terms.

BELOW LEFT: "Black Shadow" is Alby Olver's Top 20 winning '32 Ford roadster that was driven all the way from Victoria for the Nationals.

BELOW: A '55 Mercury Monterey that is all class and owned by Colin Chapman. Pearl green paintwork and whitewall tyres on chrome wheels suit perfectly.

ASRF SR NATS

ABOVE: Travis Heap owns this classy red '48 Mercury ute that features tan upholstery and chromed billet five spoke wheels.

ABOVE: Ford Y block power in a '34 Chevy Tudor isn't common but it suits Rodney Cahill from Biggenden/Piston Broke Rodders.

BELOW: Colourful line up is led by a pair of glowing Chevys, the gold roadster of Eric Gropp in the foreground features a tunnel ram equipped small block V8 engine and the candy red with overlaid flames version of John and Dee Zammit in the background that is also small block V8 powered.

BOTTOM LEFT: Bright green pearl paint makes Mark Muller's 1932 Ford Tudor stand out during the show and shine display.

BOTTOM RIGHT: Paul McMullin is a member of Deuces Limited, Queensland and enjoys nothing more than cruising with wife, Kate in their superb Model A.

LEFT: The orange '34 Chevrolet Tudor is owned by Alwin Davies while the purple '34 Chev roadster belongs to Ian McCallum. Both are members of the Emerald Car Club.

BELOW: Steven Dupond keeps right on cruising in his delightful '32 Ford three window hiboy coupe despite a heavy downpour of rain. The main pic shows Deon Willcox taking a turn to go cruising in Steve's Deuce.

BOTTOM: Crowds streamed into the showgrounds in large numbers.

ABOVE LEFT: Smooth looking FJ Holden inspired custom coupe was entered by Wesley Giles. Available as a kit based car this version is sure to become very popular.

ABOVE RIGHT: Blown flathead engine up front and loads of nostalgic style set the mood for Nick Rees'' 32 Ford hiboy roadster, complete with drag racing number and speed equipment stickers.

BELOW INSET: Daniel Keepkie entered this bright yellow American Graffiti look-alike coupe with Ford running gear and reflective firewall.

BELOW: Dean Wilson is the owner of this smart looking '34 Chevy Tudor that features mint green paintwork and stylish billet wheels. As usual, Shannons stepped up in a big way as major sponsors of the Nationals.

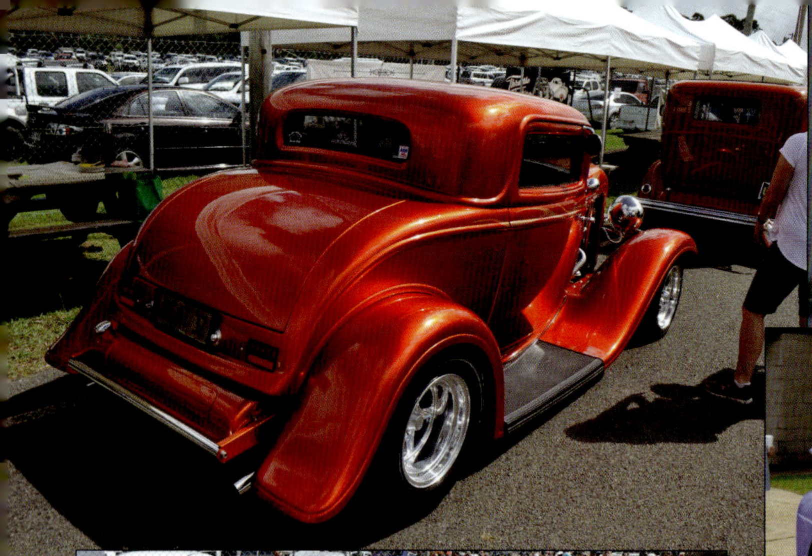

LEFT: You can't ignore Geoff Crawhall's rich candy Tangerine pearl Deuce three window coupe from the Conrodders Hot Rod & Custom Club.

BELOW LEFT: Fighter plane theme is evident on Rodney Brewer's wire wheeled '34 coupe that uses a Rod Bods slant chopped body.

BELOW: A chopped top and nicely detailed bodywork are standout features of Jeffrey Van Bakel's '42 Ford jailbar pickup.

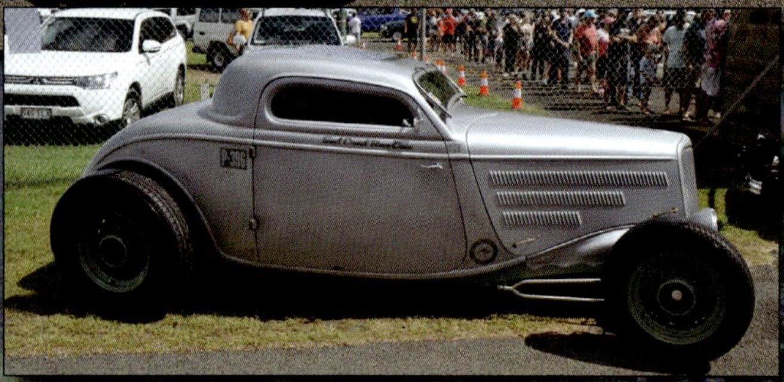

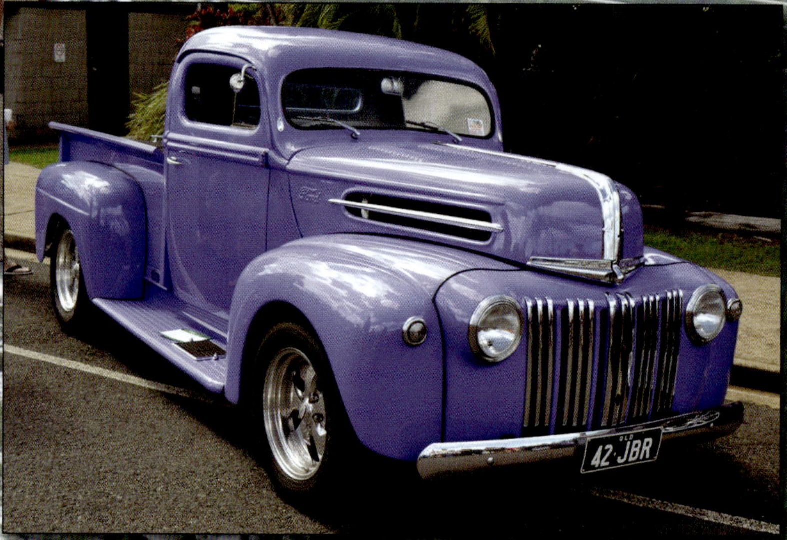

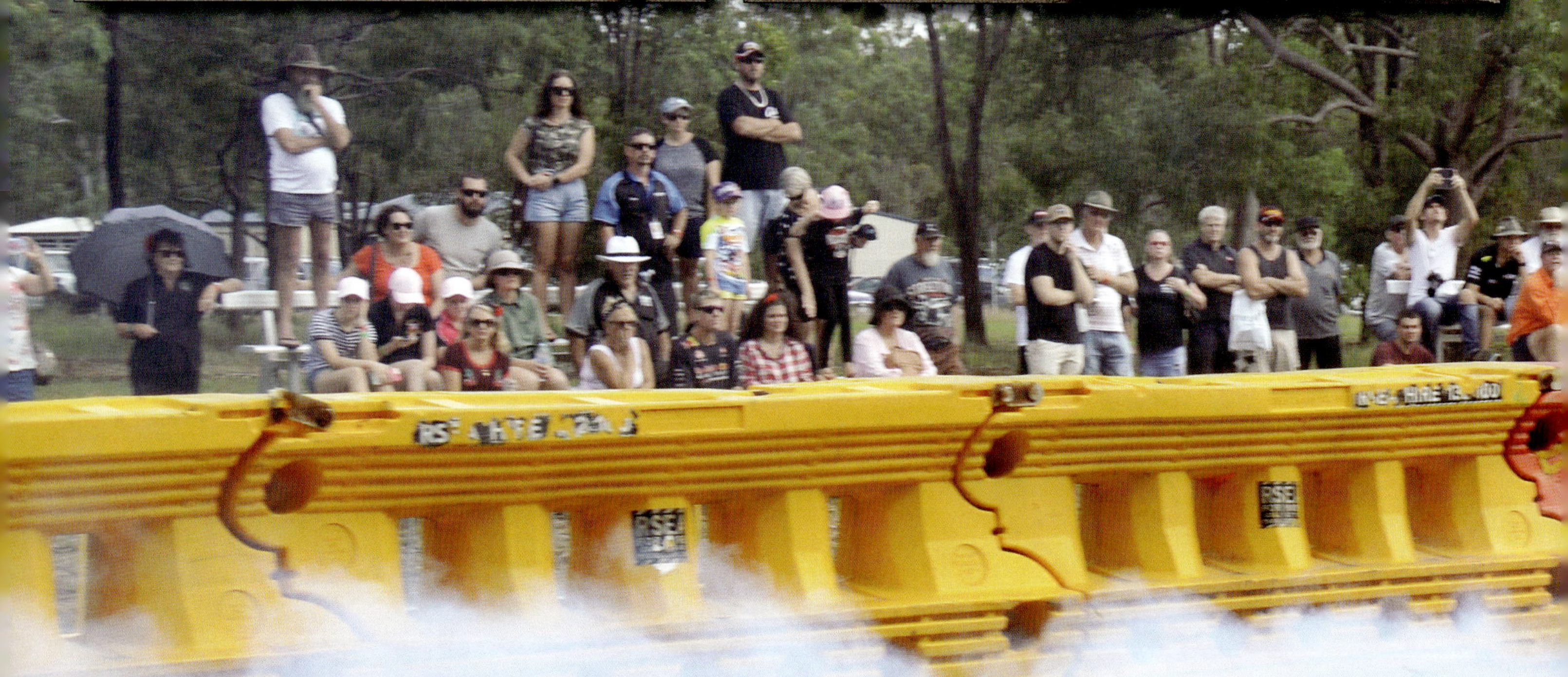

BELOW: Built many years ago by Warren Burggraaff, this '34 Chevy two door sedan features wild licking flames by custom painting aficionado Hans Kruezen. Both hail from the Rockhampton district.

BELOW: Right there amongst the Top 20 winners was Paul Connoly's '47 International tow truck. Superbly finished with murals over glossy black paintwork, the super detailed hauler is diesel powered.

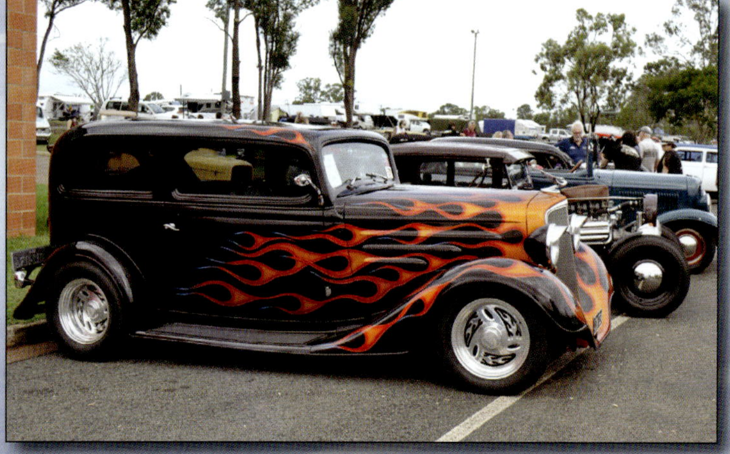

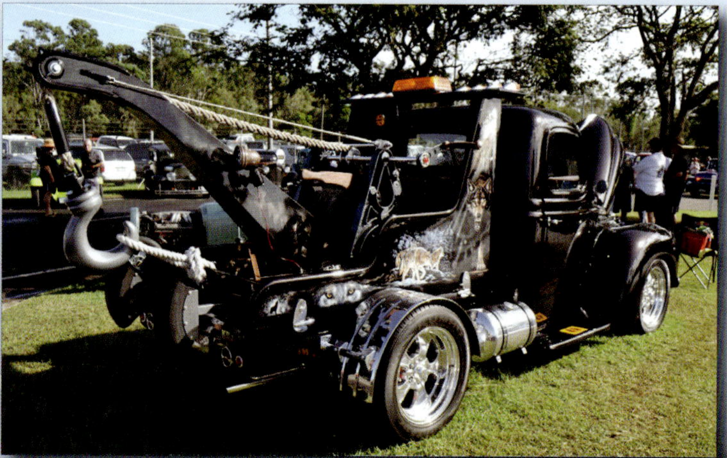

ABOVE: Ross Mayes brought his potent blown big block Chevy powered Deuce Tudor up from Victoria and went home with the winner's trophy for the men's Go-Whoa competition. Ross' Deuce is big block Chevy powered.

ABOVE: Phillip Heathwood started with an old '44 Ford pickup truck and turned it into this fad styled hot rod that uses Chrysler Hemi power and rolls on American five spoke wheels.

ABOVE: Gavin Cass makes some smoke during the Go-Whoa competition in his blown '36 Ford two door sedan that has a mild top chop and some custom body changes such as the flip open fuel filler and '35 Ford taillights. Note the third brake light in the rear window that has its own custom grille treatment, that's attention to detail!

ABOVE LEFT & LEFT: Alister Spong's '42 jailbar Ford truck might look down and out but check out the engine bay where there's a potent turbocharged late model Falcon six. Talk about a sleeper!

ABOVE RIGHT: There are lots of individual styling cues incorporated into George Berry's track T with removable hard top, upside down Jaguar grille and custom hood scoop.

MAIN PIC: Shane Springer leads this procession of cruisers in his brutish '41 Willys coupe, followed by Chris Hadgkiss' much travelled gasser style '40 Willys coupe and Ross Mayes in his flamed Deuce Tudor.

ABOVE LEFT: Having fun at the Nationals is easy when you have your own custom built mini rod based on a '41 Willys pickup like Daryl Martin.

LEFT: Scott Askew's one-of-a-kind pickup truck is based on a '35 Bedford with custom made pickup bed and fully dressed, tunnel ram equipped small block Chevy engine. Wild set of silver flames over red paintwork means you won't miss it on the highway!

ASRF SR NATS

ABOVE: Kerry Wright from the Satellite City Street Rod Club in Victoria has owned her full custom FJ Holden hardtop for many years and it has recently been treated to a rebuild and repaint. Two door conversion and custom grille with DeSoto style insert are other examples of its outstanding custom features.

ABOVE: Neat and tidy '23 T bucket was well presented by owner Arthur Tonkin, a member of Rods Inc Queensland. Arthur chose a small block Chevy to power the diminutive T and lets everyone know who belongs in which set by the little signs added to the lower section of the windscreen frame.

ABOVE: Heavy showers of rain meant Damien Emery's '32 roadster needed a top in a hurry, but the cruising didn't stop.
ABOVE RIGHT: Darryl Martin has recently rebuilt his super low profile T roadster.
RIGHT: A Top 20 trophy was awarded to Graham Blair for his fabulous, six wheel equipped 1934 Buick Victoria that rolls on American Racing five spoke wheels.

ABOVE: Deuces Limited club member, Joshua Case wowed the crowd with his just finished in time 1929 Model A Ford roadster. The red beauty sits down snug over the tyres in typical Case family fashion and features stock headlights on a dropped headlight bar, further accentuating the low stance.

ABOVE: It's been done a couple of years now, but John Philpot's channelled and Chevy powered '32 Ford pickup still stops people in their tracks.
RIGHT: Bright yellow '37 Ford pickup with '35 Ford grille belongs to Ian Hickey.

ABOVE: Glossy black paint and red interior trim always works well on a '36 Ford, especially when its a desirable, chopped three window coupe like this one owned by Richard Smeman with Corvette running gear.

ABOVE: How do you like your hiboy Deuce coupe? Blue with alloy wheels or red with steelies. The blue one belongs to engine, Tim Bartrop while Frank Fanning of Paradise Cruisers owns the red example.

ABOVE: Scalloped '32 Ford hiboy roadster is a different twist on a paint style made popular by the So-Cal roadster. This one is finished in blue and beige and sat on steel wheels with whitewall tyres.
ABOVE RIGHT: Low profile roadster pickup is based on a '27 Dodge and owned by Ken Turnbull.

ABOVE: Another Top 20 winner was the fading green, Cadillac inspired '52 Chevy delivery of Nigel Shieles.
BELOW: Beale & Kids Motorsports brought along their '37 Chevy ramp truck with sleeper cab and raw finished alminium engine hood.
RIGHT: The rocker cover racing attracted a large field of competitors, shown here lined up under the grandstand where the races took place.

ABOVE: Tank Fairlane rear components give Gavin Stevens' hot rod a style all of its own. The cowl is '30 Model A Ford and the engine is a Ford flathead behind a beer barrel Ford truck grille.

ABOVE LEFT: Justin Stoddard won a Top 20 spot for his 1934 Ford coupe.

ABOVE: Dean Wilson's 1937 Plymouth coupe was the popular winner of Top Car of the Nationals. The outstanding '37 Plymouth coupe was started by Dean's father over 10 years ago and finished in top fashion by Dean after his passing. Peter Prange from Rum City Rod & Customs entered the '32 Ford closed cab pickup with blown Hemi driveline.

ABOVE: Peter Gill's '48 Ford pickup and Lindsay Greenwood's '38 Ford sedan both came over from Tasmania while Peter Harben's '40 Ford Standard Tudor is a local Queensland car.

COLIN FREEMAN (OLSKOOL DESIGN)

When I was 16 I got to meet airbrush artist Frank Lee through my mother, they were friends. He's my idol. I've drawn for as long as I can remember and at 50 that's good going. I won "Expression Session" in Street Machine magazine, scored a set of new tyres from that in 2003. I've been lucky to love what I do. People like Aidan Donald and Mal Black I'm glad to call friends and they inspire me a lot. Over the last five years I've seen my art improve, so I'm very grateful and satisfied with life as a whole. I moved from Sydney to Palmwoods on the Queensland's Sunshine Coast and I love living there. Rick's Garage is just down the road, how lucky am I? Through my artwork I have learned that if you believe in yourself, life will reward you more than you can imagine.

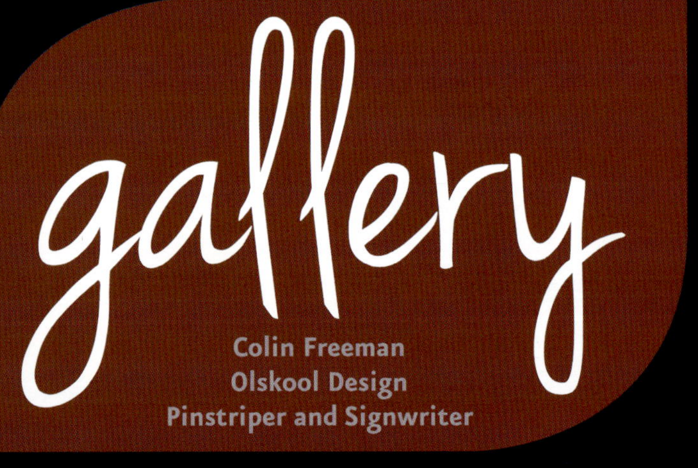

gallery

Colin Freeman
Olskool Design
Pinstriper and Signwriter

LEFT: "Good As" HQ Monaro.

ABOVE: Shoebox Red Devil.

BELOW LEFT: Nova.

RIGHT: Wild Child.

BELOW: Hot Rod.

ABOVE: Ford 32 Deuce.

BELOW: GMC 1956.

ABOVE: Zsa Zsa 1932 Ford coupe.

BELOW: Smooth, Shane Harvey HZ Holden ute.

ABOVE: Off its Nut, 1962 Holden EK Delivery.

BELOW: Dean Wilson 1937 Plymouth coupe.

Royce Everett
Auckland, New Zealand
1932 Ford Roadster
Words & Photos: Larry O'Toole

All '32 Fords look the same. Nobody dares do anything different with a '32 Ford these days. There are a couple of sweeping statements for you to ponder while you take a look over the pictures of Royce Everett's amazing '32 Ford roadster. One glance and you know those generalisations don't hold true any more. Here's a Deuce roadster that breaks the mould when it comes to building them in the tried and true traditional manner. This one is entirely scratch-built by Mac's Speed Shop in Auckland, New Zealand."

Graeme McNeill is the name behind the Mac's establishment and he started out with a Rodbods steel reproduction body and changed everything from there, taking as long as it took – until it was finished.

Of course the body needed a solid foundation under it so Graeme started that part of the project with a custom made chassis that has been stretched three inches in the wheelbase, fully boxed and had a centre K-member manufactured to suit. When ready it was powder primed and painted silver/coco brown to match the finished overall paint scheme.

Up front is a Magnum four inch dropped, drilled and chromed I-beam axle sitting under a chromed transverse leaf spring assisted by Bilstein gas tube shock absorbers. The front brakes are hydraulic early Ford items fitted with Buick finned brake drums and Wilson Welding finned '39 Ford backing plates. Royce and Graeme combined their talents to make the custom pedal system that brings the brakes into play, working on another set of Buick finned drum equipped early Ford brakes with '39 Ford backing plates on the 31 spline original Halibrand magnesium quick-change rear end that was rebuilt by Mac's Speed Shop. Bilstein gas tube shock absorber are also used on the rear end together with '35-'48 rear lower shock mounts as manufactured by Mac's Speed Shop.

Setting the directions for the roadster is a cowl mounted Schroeder sprint car steering box with ratio doubler, topped with a Moto-Lita steering wheel imported from England.

The chassis rolls on custom 16 inch spoke front wheels that have been black powder coated and fitted with Excelsior Competition 5.50x16 radial tyres and custom knock off style hub caps made by MAC's Speed Shop. The rear wheels are the same style of custom made spokes with 7.00x18 Excelsior Competition radial tyres and knock-off caps.

That Hemi engine is a Chrysler 343 cubic inch variation fitted with mechanical Hilborn fuel injection that has been converted to electronic operation by Mac's Speed Shop, plus a custom made Pro-coated and chromed exhaust system. Absorbing the torque from that substantial Hemi engine is a Chrysler New Process A833 four speed gearbox with a Hurst Competition Plus shifter modified to centre operation. A Bob Drake 12 gallon reproduction fuel tank holds the fuel that is sent forward through #6 black braided fuel lines by a Holley electric fuel pump.

Creating a Deuce roadster with a difference means the body didn't

Mac's speed Shop scratch-build a roadster for Royce Everett

escape without some serious reworking too. The stock '32 firewall was modified and reinforced to suit the cowl mounted steering and it has been fitted with burst-proof bear claw door latches. A curved and chopped wiperless windscreen with special bronze stanchions was supplied by Stanley Wanlass while the custom brown canvas top came from Dick Rodwell.

When all the changes had been completed, Scott Tercel of ST Bodyworks in Auckland prepared it all for Antonievich Restoration of Pukekohe to lay on the custom Porsche Silver paint with Cocoa tinter. Only then did Ian Goodwin go to work on the interior trim using Porsche Cocoa brown leather over a custom bucket style bench seat and brown German loop pile carpet on the floor. Custom inner door handles are another example of parts custom made by Mac's Speed Shop. The same brown leather and carpet trim is used in the trunk and it hides the custom made wiring harness.

A custom dash panel is another Mac's Speed Shop fabricated component that is fitted with Stewart Warner electric gauges while the lights, ignition and battery switches are mounted under the seat. Turn signals are integrated into the 1936 Packard headlights that have also been modified to accept H4 inserts and the taillights are 1936 DeSoto items with custom chrome spine and glass, again with LED indicators incorporated.

Other features of this highly individual Deuce roadster include the use of ARP fasteners throughout, a MOON radiator overflow tank and a 12V Powermaster Power Generator.

Chrome plating was carried out by Bumper Replacement New Zealand and the engine is the work of Papakura Engine Specialists, Murray Smith, Auckland.

RØYSTR

RØYSTR

RØYSTR

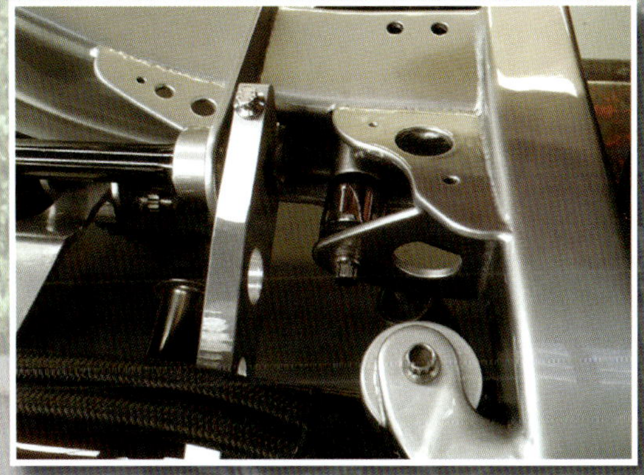

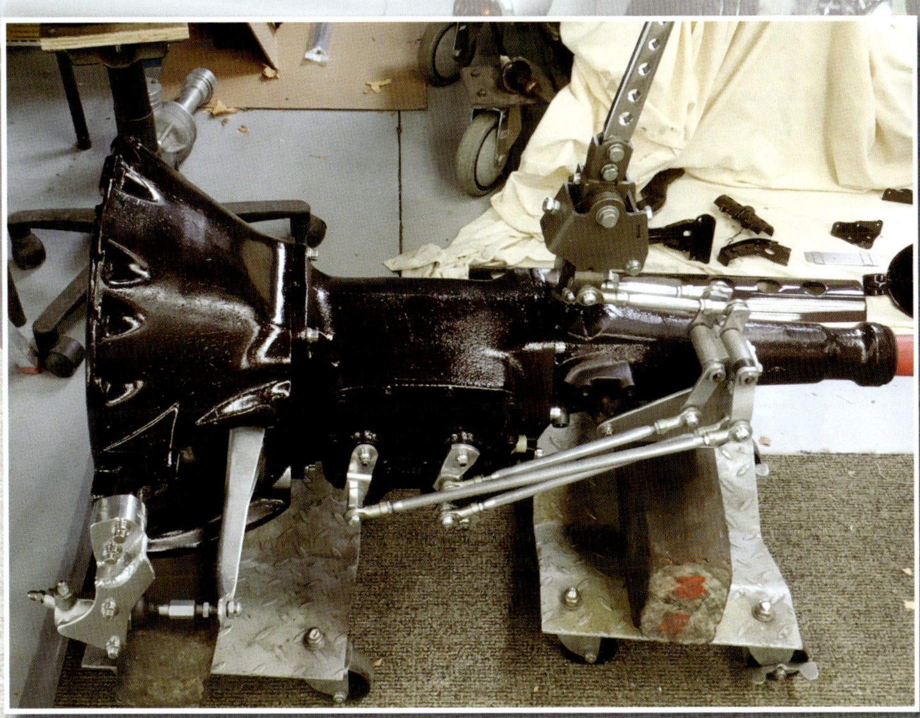

ABOVE: Greg Weld's '40 Ford pickup is an absolute stunner that was built by Customs & Hot Rods of Andile with Don Hardy built 550HP LS3 engine, PPG Paint, Roadster Shop chassis.

MAIN PIC: A bright red '70 Pontiac GTO convertible leads this group of award winners to the presentation area on the Sunday.

LEFT: "Maybellene" is a unique 1958 custom Lincoln Continental MKIII owned by Ted and Sue Leach that was extensively modified by Kindigit Design, has a 600 cubic inch supercharged V12 engine and interior trim by JS Custom Interiors.

Northwest Nationals ★

GOODGUYS ROD & CUSTOM ASSOCIATION COOL CARS, COOL PEOPLE, COOL TIMES

Words & Photos: Larry O'Toole

BELOW: Rick and Alta Steele from Post Falls showed off their 1952 Chevrolet Belair that runs a tri-power 350 Chevy engine and 200R4 auto transmission.

BOTTOM: The '39 Buick coupe belongs to Alexandra and Galen Pavliska. It is 327 Chevy powered and painted Cool Ruby Red. Judi and Bill Desnan, Spokane Valley, WA own the two tone '38 Ford Standard coupe that uses 350/350 Chevy running gear.

The Goodguys Street Rod Association hosts a string of events across the north American continent, culminating in their Goodguys Nationals in Columbus in mid-summer each year. These regional events are great opportunities to compare hot rodding in the different parts of the USA and see how they compare with each other. This was the first time I had attended the Pacific North West Nationals and I was lucky enough to be at the biggest and best one yet held at the Washington State Fairground in Puyallup, just outside Seattle.

This Fairground is quite large and it was almost filled to capacity with rods, customs and classics from the 1920s to the 1980s. The layout is such that there are hidden pockets throughout the venue leading to surprises for the casual visitor as you keep finding another corner filled with cars you haven't seen yet.

Not far inside the main gate there is a large building that houses the commercial traders and it is surrounded by more high performance businesses that have their own trading set ups outside. The entrant cars are then sprinkled right throughout the rest of the facility, up and down the laneway-like access roads and gathered together here and there in the several open spaces. One of these spaces also acts as the venue for a small swap meet and another for the various "show within a show" specialist gatherings such as "You Gotta Drive 'Em" and "Builders Showcase".

The Seattle area is notorious for having a fairly wet climate but July, when the Puyallup event is staged, is the driest month of the year. For the 2019 version the weather was just about perfect all weekend, fine, mostly sunny but not too hot. As a result there were thousands of spectators there, particularly on the Saturday when the number of cars present is also at its peak of 2800 entries.

By early afternoon on the Sunday the show starts winding down with 75 awards presented in drive-through style to bring it all to a conclusion. If you are in the Pacific North West of the USA in the future, mark the last full weekend of July on your calendar for a must-do to take in the Goodguys Pacific North West Nationals. ■

LEFT: Steve Albert brought along his '39 Ford beer barrel cab-over truck with his equally attractive '46 Solar midget racer on the back. The midget uses a worked V8-60 flathead and Halibrand quick-change rear end. The truck uses flathead Ford V8 running gear with a Gear Vendors overdrive. Orting, WA is home.

ABOVE: It's always worth a visit to the swap meet section.

RIGHT: "Li'l Tug Boat" is Martina and Darren Hoffman's snub nosed COE based Cameo pickup that is powered by a Gibbs Racing 409 Chevy engine that has been stroked to 472! Other features include an Art Morrison back half and Mustang II front end.

MAIN PIC: Entrants line up to register on arrival at the Puyallup Fairgrounds venue on Friday. This line up is indicative of the variety of vehicle styles and eras that attend the Goodguys North West Nationals held in late July each year.

TOP LEFT: Chuck Miller of Longview, WA owns this desirable '62 Chrysler 300 that sits low to the ground and runs a 413 cubic inch engine with 727 Torqueflite automatic transmission.

ABOVE: Locals Robin and Paula Ordonez attended in their '32 Ford roadster pickup. The scalloped Deuce uses '53 Mercury engine hooked to a '36 Ford manual transmission. It's a typical '50s hot rod with vintage speed equipment.

TOP RIGHT: Two examples of early '70s Chevy square body vehicles, a Suburban and a Pickup, models that have suddenly become very popular in the hot rod and custom movement.

ABOVE: Gasser style Willys pickup is owned by Mick Strub from nearby Tacoma, WA. Mick's pickup is a '41 model with 371 cubic inch Olds engine and four speed manual transmission.

RIGHT: This one exhibited absolute class from end to end. Russ Moen of Port Albenni, BC entered the '54 Chevrolet Tourliner that he custom built using a Cummins diesel engine with automatic transmission. Inside the back is fully kitted out as a mobile home with high quality timber finish throughout. Even the cabin is fitted out to luxury car standard with lift up floor to access the engine.

BELOW: Bringing a smile to the faces of everyone in attendance was Brent Mills with his '59 Zar Car, a one-off concept vehicle that looked like something straight out of the Jetsons television series.

BELOW LEFT: How about a '69 International Scout rebuilt as a custom car? This one was entered by Scott Nixon from Rochester, WA.

BOTTOM LEFT: Kyle Wick showed us it doesn't have to be mainstream to be a classy custom. This is his 1960 Mercury.

BELOW: Ken Adams, Bremertin, WA owns this '47 Studebaker that's fitted with a 350 Chevy engine.

BOTTOM: Bob and Sarah Davidson own the Living Legend '50 Ford Club Coupe that is powered by a flathead V8.

ABOVE: Rich from Seabeck, WA advises passengers to "Hang On" when riding in his '48 Anglia thanks to a 355 Chevy engine with five speed transmission.

RIGHT: Two years work went into Ron Potts' '68 Chevy C10 long bed pickup. The stylish truck features two tone PPG paint, a big block 454 Chevy engine and Flowmaster exhaust. Home for Ron is Auburn, WA.

ABOVE: Classy '30 Model A Ford Tudor with two tone paint scheme, chopped top, set back 460 Ford engine and five speed Tremec transmission belongs to Harvey Prato, Armstrong, BC.

ABOVE: Bill and Debbie Scherrer outfitted this '33 Ford cabriolet with ZZ502 big block Chevy running gear and a nine inch Ford rear end. The airbrushed flames are by Larry Fator of Quicksilver Speed and Color.

LEFT: Perky looking '29 Chevy truck is powered by a 1991 TPI 350 Chevy V8 with Turbo 350 transmission and has Heidts independent front suspension. It was designed and built by Si Pellow from Graham, WA.

BELOW LEFT: Jerry Logan's dumped on the ground '57 Ford has 351 Cleveland, chopped top and has been nosed and decked. A cool ride in anybody's language. Jerry hails from Toledo, WA.

BELOW: You can't miss Daryl Dinwiddie's yellow and black '57 Ford that resides at Tacoma, WA. Under the hood is a supercharged engine, just the thing for cruising the Puyallup Fairgrounds.

BELOW: It only seems right that there would be some Cal style VW beetles in amongst the scores of hot rods and custom cars at Puyallup.

ABOVE: We don't see enough centre door T sedans like this green example caught cruising the fairgrounds and showing off its polished Jag rear end.

BELOW: Classy classics glide by each other on the way in and out of the fairgrounds. The copper and white '55 DeSoto is owned by Alan Britz of Renton, WA while the two tone blue Olds coupe is a desirable '50 model "Rocket 88" coupe.

BELOW: Jack Crawford's Jumpin Jack Flash severely chopped '34 Ford coupe with 392 Hemi power has been on the scene for a while but always makes you stop and look one more time.

Goodguys Nats

LEFT: There were some rapid rods at the Friday night drags, including this bronze Deuce Tudor running off an index of 8.65.

BELOW: Would have loved to see this Thunderbird doorslammer make a full pass, it was clocking easy six second times with only little better than half strip passes on full power – a really rapid race car!

INSET BELOW: "Strip Teaser' is a yellow '55 Chevy gasser that looks like it could have been racing 50 years ago but it was just as content cruising the Puyallup Fairgrounds.

BELOW: Immediately recognisable is the Gene Winfield fade-away paint scheme on John Foxley's chopped, channelled and sectioned '52 Chevy custom that was built on a Malibu frame. Chrome wheels with whitewall tyres finish it off perfectly. Home for John is Pitt Meadows, BC.

ABOVE: Bradford's Fiat Topolino altered reverses to the start line after a burnout at the Friday night nostalgia drags.

ABOVE: It's hard not to like Gene Quanz's '60 Ford F100 with its outstanding yellow paint and a 435 small block Ford engine under the hood.

BELOW: A '32 Victoria style Buick coupe was never made by the factory so Keith Bingham of Covington, WA, made his own and equipped it with an LTI 350 Chevy engine.

BELOW RIGHT: Superb red Model A roadster on '32 rails with tunnel ram equipped Hemi engine is owned by Roger Beer of Auburn, WA.

ABOVE: Rob Campbell's '64 Falcon runs a 200ci engine with aftermarket aluminium 2V head similar to those fitted to Australian Falcons from the late seventies, but with fuel injection ports added.

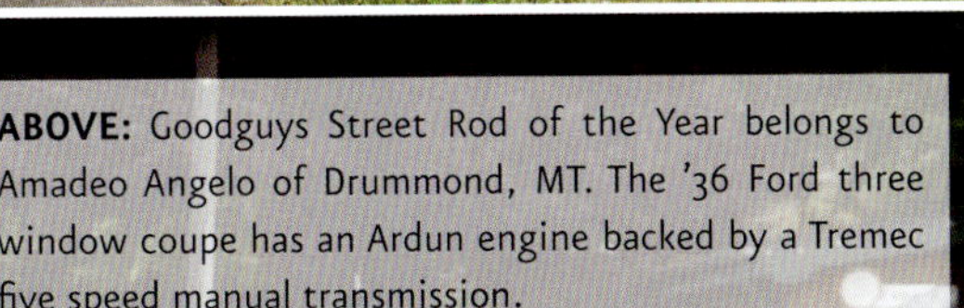

ABOVE: Goodguys Street Rod of the Year belongs to Amadeo Angelo of Drummond, MT. The '36 Ford three window coupe has an Ardun engine backed by a Tremec five speed manual transmission.

ABOVE: Cool looking '32 full fendered roadster was entered by Judy and Bill Sivak from Harrison Hot Springs, BC. The very tidy Deuce runs a 351 Ford engine and features a dropped headlight bar, along with a perfect fitting top.

ABOVE: Keith Simmonds' 572 big block Chevy powered '55 Chevy convertible shares parking space with the red 1955 DeSoto convertible of Rod Sutton that has 291 Hemi, Powerflite auto transmission – one of 625 made.

RIGHT: Think this '39 Ford coupe owned by Tom and Jane Harris' looks a little different? The body has been sectioned 1-7/8 inches, hood sectioned and peaked, '41 Studebaker taillights fitted and '40 Ford door handles moved to the trim line.

BELOW: Larry Fuller used a combination of other parts to build his '35 International pickup. The cab and grille are original items but the fenders and running boards are '34 Ford.

ABOVE: Giveaway car for Goodguys in 2016 was this Mike Goldman Customs built white '32 Ford hiboy roadster that was won by Dennis Brazer.
ABOVE RIGHT: Only a '74 VW Thing could be this much fun to cruise the fairgrounds in. Taylor Clark brought it from Victoria, BC. Note the old road signs used as a floor!
BELOW: Jim and Dana Linton's hand built '37 Ford pickup displays a healthy, blown 392 Hemi engine and Tremec five speed transmission.

ABOVE: "Daddys Olds" belongs to Kevin Dagel, Kirkland, WA. It's a '38 Oldsmobile, two door sedan with 403 V8 engine and air bag suspension.
ABOVE RIGHT: Slick looking '58 Chevy Apache Fleetside pickup of Dave Boudewin features a hard tonneau and chromed Rallye wheels. Victoria, BC is home.
RIGHT: Olson and Wayne Dixon parked their retro style '39 Chevy and '45 GMC pickups together for maximum impact.

LEFT: Line up of Willys coupes includes the purple '41 with blown 383 Chevy small block owned by Tom Noon, Kirkland, WA, the blue and silver '41 with 392 Hemi of Rick Willams from Bonney Lake, WA and the black '41 with 632 cubic inch big block Chevy owned by Satoshi Yamamoto from Bellevue, WA.

ABOVE: One of the smallest vehicles ever sold in the USA was the Crossley from the early '50s. Just the thing to paint satin black and rework into a Coca Cola service vehicle for cruising the Puyallup Fairgrounds.

ABOVE: Mike Moice owns this individual '47 Diamond T truck that has been turned into a large pickup. The practical vehicle is 327 Chevy powered and has polished checker plate lining the bed area.

ABOVE: Bud Wolfe from Garam, WA surprised everyone with his rare '60 Edsel convertible, the only one I have ever seen!. Low stance and clean styling make it an outstanding custom classic vehicle.

BELOW: Tim Wilcox drives his channelled '30 Model A Ford coupe like he stole it. The coupe uses Olds 394/700R4 running gear and hails from Abbotsford, BC.

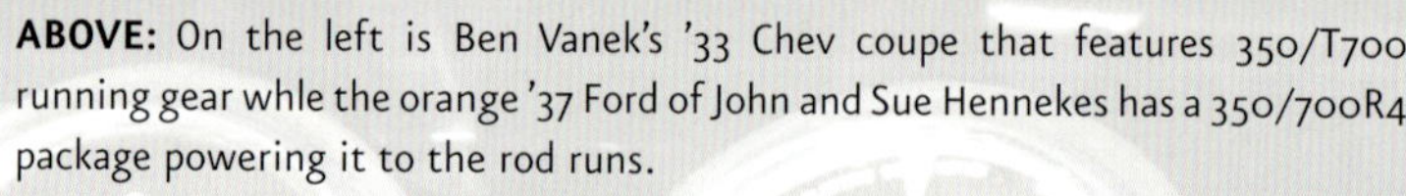

ABOVE: On the left is Ben Vanek's '33 Chev coupe that features 350/T700 running gear whle the orange '37 Ford of John and Sue Hennekes has a 350/700R4 package powering it to the rod runs.

ABOVE: No question this '76 Chevette has enough power to get the job done. That's a blown 572 cubic inch big block Chevy engine stuffed in the engine bay that powers the car to low 8 second passes at the drags!

ABOVE: Couldn't you have some fun in this cut down Model A if you paid the 20K asking price and drove it away? The "turtledeck roadster" appears to have been cut down from a Briggs bodied '28 Model A Ford four door sedan body.

ABOVE: Contrasting red and black paint scheme on Jim Beckworth's '50 Chevy coupe makes it stand out. Running gear consists of 350/350 Chevy.

ABOVE: A few specials from the swap meet include these rocker covers for Thunderbird special $125.00, Thunderbird finned alloy for $500.00 and Edmunds for $600.00.
BELOW: Project '47 Ford pickup looks to be fairly well under way and probably good buying at $14,500.00 obo.

ABOVE: Left is an early Edelbrock Victor big block Chevy single four barrel tunnel ram manifold for $525.00. On the right is a 270 cubic inch Dodge Red Ram engine with complete gasket set and triple carb intake but in need of pistons for $1000.00 complete.

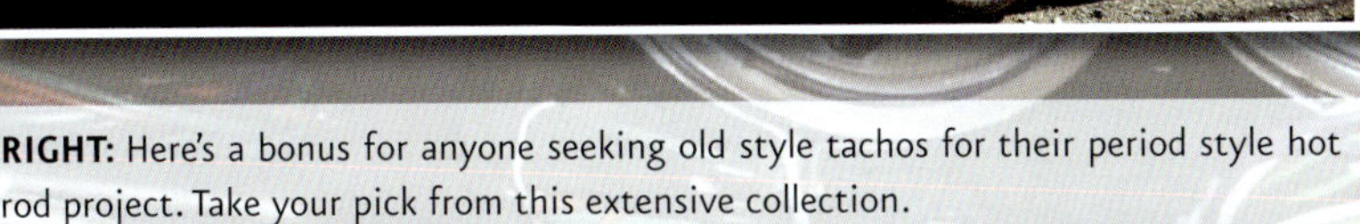

RIGHT: Here's a bonus for anyone seeking old style tachos for their period style hot rod project. Take your pick from this extensive collection.

ABOVE: There was no chassis with this '48 Studerbaker pickup cabin but it did come with the original fenders and was in very good original condition. It was advertised as available to the best offer.

ABOVE: This '36 Ford sedan had been in storage for the last 40 years and came with Chevy 327 engine, Turbo 350 trans, Ford nine inch rear end, and coil spring front suspension for $8000.00 obo in cash.

ABOVE LEFT & LEFT: Chris and Angela Church brought their '40 Ford pickup from Oregon City, OR. It uses LS3 Chevy engine, 4L80E transmission and sits on the ground thanks to air bag suspension.

ABOVE: Jim Malone's '54 Oldsmobile 98 Covertible came from Farmingotn, NM using LS3 Chevy engine, 4L70 transmision, Fatman stub axles, air-ride suspension and PPG Vibrance Sunset Red paint. The interior features Ron Magnus leather, the wheels are Billet Specialties and the steering column came from Ididit.

ABOVE: Behind that graceful Deuce grille is an 8BA flathead engine in Doug Grande's '30 Model A Ford hiboy roadster. Cruising past is Paul Smith from Puyallup, WA in his '27 T Ford roadster that is powered by an Olds/Cadillac V8 engine.

BELOW: A blown 392 cubic inch Chrysler Hemi engine with six speed transmission powers Cal Stewart's '32 Ford hiboy roadster. Unfinished interior trim indicates Jim's roadster is a work in progress.

ABOVE: Don Sangster of Wenatchee, WA entered his superb '32 Ford Fordor sedan that sports a Buick V8, five speed manual transmission and amazing attention to detail throughout.

ABOVE: Dave and Marci Krogh, Tacoma, WA entered their unique monotone '28 Dodge coupe that sports a chopped top and painted artillery style wheels.
RIGHT: Adam Perkerewicz from Gig Harbor WA owns this very rare '37 Ford sedan delivery that runs a 350/350 combination and artillery style wheels.

ABOVE: Who would have thought a '39 Ford panel truck could look so good when given the street rod treatment? Irene and Don Richardson, that's who.

T.R.O.G.
Santa Barbara DRAGS

ABOVE: Chopped Deuce coupes of Jay Dean and Dean Micetich, both ex-pat Englishmen now hot rodding in southern California.

ABOVE: Jimmy White from Circle City Hot Rods brought along his Hemi powered Model A coupe and his 1942 Harley Davidson to race at T.R.O.G.

Robert Genat's book "The Birth of Hot Rodding" was the inspiration for the resurgence of the "Oilers Car Club" and ultimately the West Coast version of The Race of Gentlemen. That led to a meeting with Oilers founder Jim Nelson who suggested the promoters of The Race of Gentlemen take over the Oilers Club and keep the movement going. There have been previous Races of Gentlemen in Wildwood, New Jersey and Pismo Beach, California but the West Coast version went to Santa Barbara for 2019, where the race was held on Cabrillo Avenue, right alongside the city's East Beach.

A 660 feet drag strip with the same amount of braking area was set up on the avenue with the pits located in the parking lot of the Hilton Hotel. As you can imagine, getting that sort of arrangement passed by city officials wasn't without its moments, but the event went ahead and The Race of Gentlemen was a huge success.

Based on racing as it was back then, there are criteria that entrant vehicles have to meet to keep it all "in the era" so most of the race cars are based on old jalopy style hot rods as you can see in the photos. To qualify to enter, motorcycles have to be pre-1947 and cars pre-1953. Safety wasn't an issue back then, to the same extent it is today, but somehow flame-proof suits and massive roll cages just don't suit the theme, so drivers were advised to dress for the period, think of their families and treat their own safety accordingly. It worked! This type of racing is all about fun, winning or losing doesn't matter.

Most of the competitors are from the younger generations of hot rodders, but they certainly have the blessing of the original competitors who looked on with satisfied smiles, knowing yet another generation was enjoying the thrill of racing their hot rods, the same way they did 70 years ago.

ABOVE: Japanese hot rodder, Atsushi Yasui shipped his narrowed T modified roadster over to the USA from Tokyo to race at both east and west coast T.R.O.G. events.

ABOVE: Alex Carlos in his "Penny Hemi" 1927 T Ford coupe versus Charles Chavez from the Emperors of Victorville in his Model A roadster pickup, "Emperors Brew". Alex's coupe runs a 354 cubic inch Hemi topped with a Weiand intake and six carbies while Charles' roadster pickup uses a 324 cubic inch Oldsmobile engine that was built by Iskenderian in the 1960s.

RIGHT: Mike Thompson from Ridgefield, Washington rolls with the Estranged Car Club and owns this wicked Deuce three window coupe. It was chopped by Barris and upholstered by Gaylord's Kustom Tops in 1951 and street raced in So-Cal by Don Rackemann and Joe Pisano in the late fifties and early sixties. It was repainted in 1981 and now runs a Cragar supercharger and triple carbs atop a 1961 283 Chevy with a four speed.

ABOVE: Customs by the Sea featuring the incredible Rotunda of Customs display inside the Hilton Santa Barbara Beachfront Resort and on the trackside spectator lawn. Across the centre of the page we have Burbank Choppers member Jon "Fish" Fisher's chopped '36 Ford three window coupe with '40 LaSalle grille, 1939 Buick headlights, '41 Ford bumpers and a '37 Lincoln Zephyr dash, John Denich's Larry Watson "Grapevine" clone '50 Chevy with '55 Olds side trim and '53 Chevy grille teeth and Kelly and Mark Skipper's chopped '51 Ford, "Royal Victoria" that also features '53 Chevy grille teeth and '54 Dodge side trim.

BELOW: The Model A coupe is an old hot rod that was built by Rod Dickinson as a teenager in Tucumcari, New Mexico back in 1961-62, and now Rattlers club member, Daniel Shircliff from Phoenix, Arizona uses it as his daily driver. It features red trim with white tuck and roll pleats, a 1957 Chev steering wheel, a padded dash, chrome garnish moulds, an aluminium firewall and a peaked roof that was filled using the hood from a 1960 Mercury. It runs a 1956 265 Chevy V8 topped with triple 97s and uses a 1940 Ford rear end. Louis Stands of the Hubcats Motor Club of Orange County owns the original steel 1927 T roadster. It is mounted on a Deuce chassis with a dropped 1932 axle up front and runs a tri-power equipped 1963 327 Corvette small block, four speed gearbox and a Dana rear end with a 1940 Ford spring. The interior features a 1940 Ford wheel and the instrument panel from a 1948 F1 pickup.

BELOW INSET: Justin Baas piloting the John Riley 1929 roadster. Riley was a founding member of the Road Runners in 1937 and this car was built in the late fifties. It appeared on the March 1959 cover of Hot Rod magazine and runs a 283 Chevy.

BELOW: All-steel 1941 Willys coupe on magnesium Halibrands is a true survivor from the past with plenty of history. The coupe was raced around the Denver area in the 1950s with Pontiac power, then Dave Mader and Jerry Morris added their names to the body and raced it with a chain-driven supercharger in the Kansas area from 1959 to 1964, when Mader was sent to Vietnam. While Mader was away, Morris pulled the motor out and took the car to a junkyard. Mike DeVriendt of Greeley, Colorado then bought the Willys from a salvage yard south of Wichita, Kansas. Randy Gribble from Lake City Rod & Custom in Watertown, South Dakota then purchased the car from DeVriendt in 1990 and installed a blown 1957 392 Hemi, Turbo 400 and 1957 Pontiac rear end. He owned the Willys for nearly 30 years before it was sold to current owner, Gil Muro of Hot Rod Ranch in Lompoc, California. Rory Forbes owns the "Little Zip" T roadster, another car with significant history.

LEFT: Vintage motorcycle enthusiasts put on a great show at T.R.O.G. Santa Barbara Drags. This scene from the pit area shows Jimmy White from Circle City Hot Rods getting ready to race his 1942 Harley Davidson while Adrian from the Odd Squad Car Club slinks through the background in his banger powered Model T Ford roadster, "The Slippery Eel".

BELOW: Jimmy White also owns this bitchin' chopped 1931 Model A Ford coupe. It rides on a shortened and narrowed 1936 Ford chassis and boasts a 334 Hemi topped with a Weiand Drag Star intake mounting six carbs, and is backed by a four speed manual transmission.

LEFT: Arie van Schyndel's chopper features purple fade paint, a 103ci Knucklehead motor, custom staggered handle bars, a devil's tail sissy bar and a chromed German military helmet oil tank, hence the bike's name, "The German Merman".

BELOW: Lars Mapstead in another genuine survivor hot rod from the fifties, "Bronze Flame". It was raced on the dry lakes and at the Santa Ana drags by original owner, Ed Donato and features its original lacquer paint, Mercury flathead running gear, plus a track nose that was fabricated by Sam Barris.

BELOW: Immortals club member, Diana Branch racing her 4.5 inch chopped '32 Ford Tudor. This channelled Deuce runs a 299ci Studebaker V8 and Tremec five speed gearbox backed by a '57 Chevy diff. It also features a '36 Ford dash.

ABOVE: Lynn Bird racing his '25 T Model speedster against Esteban Gonzalez in his '30 AV8 roadster. The T is mounted on a heavily modified '34 Chev chassis and runs a '48 Mercury flathead with Offenhauser heads and an Edmunds dual carb intake manifold.
BELOW: Joe Buffardi lined up in the staging area in his track nosed 1929 Ford Model A roadster that runs a 1949 337ci Lincoln flathead equipped with an Edmunds intake.

BELOW: Tom Franzi found this late fifties-built Model A hot rod for sale on eBay, flew over to the USA from Germany and purchased the car in Lodi, California just one week before the race. This roadster once wore metalflake green lace paint over its six inch channelled body and features a sectioned 1932 grille, a mahogany timber dash filled with Stewart Warner gauges and 1964 Dodge taillights. A 1956 324 cubic inch Oldsmobile Rocket V8 is backed by a manualised Hydromatic transmission and early Oldsmobile rear end. The roadster was shown at the Oakland Roadster Show in 1970 by the late Richard Howard. The 1930 Model A in the right lane belongs to Nick Sloatman from the Spirits Car Club.

Santa Barbara

ABOVE: Gil Muro preparing to launch his blown Hemi '41 Willys gasser.

RIGHT: El Vinos Car Club member, Jay Dean from Nostalgia Ranch entered his Navajo Brown, three and a half inch chopped Deuce five window that runs a 331 Caddy V8 and five speed 'box.

BELOW RIGHT: Sam Davis' Deuce five window coupe struggles to gain traction as Ron Cooper gets the jump in his T Model roadster.

BELOW: Jeff Seliga in his grey '31 Model A roadster versus Jim Luke in his 21 stud flathead powered '29 Model A Ford roadster.

BELOW: Rory Forbes from Reno, Nevada recently found surviving parts (body, hood and grille) of this T roadster, "Little Zip" for sale on Craigslist and thrashed for two months to get it ready for T.R.O.G. The history in this car dates back to 1949 when it was used as a circle track racer in southern California. It was then built by shop teacher, Al Morris and his class in 1958/9 with a brand new 283 Chevy V8 and ran at the 1959 NHRA National Drags in Detroit before being stored away and eventually parted out. It's a different car now with a new chassis and running gear, but still features the Joe Bailon candy apple red paint and Tommy the Greek pinstriping.

RIGHT: Justin Baas in the blue '29 roadster facing off against Nick Sloatman in the number 54 car. The '29 roadster runs a 283 Chevy in an original '32 frame and features raised and bobbed rear fenders, an original dropped axle, '40 front brakes and a later Ford rear end with buggy spring.

BELOW RIGHT: Another couple of Burbank Choppers club cars here with Deron Wright's 283 powered Deuce three window and Jack Carroll's chopped, channelled and flathead powered '32 five window.

BELOW: Dick DeLuna's Rolling Bones-built '34 Ford coupe, "Salinas Special" runs a '49 8BA Ford flathead measuring 284 cubic inches, a Chevy S-10 five-speed gearbox and a Rodsville quick-change diff. It also features a rare Canadian Cockshutt tractor grille.

ABOVE & RIGHT: Tom Branch from the Immortals CC owns the channelled Deuce roadster with 304ci Studebaker V8, Tremec five speed gearbox and '57 Chevy diff. Ex-pat Englishman, Dean Micetich owns the '55 Cadillac V8 powered Deuce three window that was painted bronze back in '64.

Saturday September 21 saw Sydney Dragway take a step back to wilder times as the Aeroflow World Fuel Altered Challenge shook the venue with the best nostalgia drag meet this country has ever seen. A huge field of entries consisting of 12 Fuel Altereds, nine Wild Bunch entries, 34 Top Modified dragsters, 11 Boosted Outlaws, 12 Pro Extreme cars and eight Extreme Bikes, along with 29 in the Street Machine bracket, seven in Hot Rod and a whopping 34 gassers fronted up to battle it out for the Vintage Gas title. There were also two Nitro Funny Cars, "Rocket Ship" and "Nitro Sherrif" putting down exhibition runs.

Making this event a tri-country world challenge were four Aussie fuel altereds from Graeme Cowin's stable, "Agro", "Berserk", "Psycho" and "Chucky's Toy", taking on four altereds from the USA while Morice McMillan in "Spooky" and Dave Gauld in "Nitemare" flew the flag for New Zealand.

Coming together from different states across the USA to be shipped over from California, the four American altereds that attended are some of the most famous of their breed, and certainly entertained the crowd every time they came onto the strip. Randy and Sue Bradford brought their AA/FA 1938 Fiat Topolino out to Sydney from Camano Island, Washington, Hughie and Shawn Callen brought their big block Chevy powered, "High Heaven" over from Boise, Idaho, Rich Guasco brought "Pure Hell" in from Pleasanton, California and Ron Hope shipped "Rat Trap" over from Franklin, Tennessee.

Dave Gauld's "Nitemare" altered was shipped over from New Zealand along with three gassers for the Vintage Gas bracket; Dave Best's "Twistin' Pistons" Model A coupe, GT Norris' "Pist 'n' Broke" 1953 Kaiser Frazer Henry J and Craig Mukllan's 1959 Studebaker Lark, "Larkness Monster". Food vans, market stalls, a static show and shine plus kids rides and entertainment gave punters plenty to do during a delay in racing, caused by Dave McGaw hitting the wall in spectacular fashion with the "Quick Cut" Supercharged Outlaw funny car. Dave walked away from the incident but the delay stretched the day out and a rain storm put an end to racing just before the final rounds.

With no clear winner discernable between the three competing countries in the World Fuel Altered Challenge, there's some unfinished business to attend to in the future. There's already plenty of talk of there being another event like this, so if and when that happens, be sure to get there, you won't be disappointed.

ABOVE: This flamed Bantam AA fuel altered was originally built by Bob and Jim Hensel of San Bruno, California. It now belongs to Sydney racer, Colin Walls.

RIGHT: Aussie, Justin Walshe in "Berzerk" gets the jump on American, Randy Bradford in his Fiat Topolino in a thrilling AA Fuel Altered run.

LEFT: The Boosted Outlaw bracket featured some wild altereds, including Darren Bazarnik's blown big block Chevy powered "Rat Trap" tribute car. The car is based on a die-cast scale replica of Ron Hope's altered and was built by Grant O'Rourke.

Story & Pics: Al O'Toole

BELOW: Andrew Hurst's Ford T bucket based altered was on display among the cacklefest cars. It features 6-71 blown, Enderle injected, nitromethane-fed 392 Chrysler Hemi power, spindle-mount 12 spoke magnesium front runners and Mickey Thompson drag slicks.

ABOVE & RIGHT: Darren Bazarnik lifting the front wheels again, this time against Andrew Hodgson in the "Avenger" funny car. Bazarnik's altered runs a supercharged 463 cubic inch big block Chevy while there's a Brad Anderson blown 526 Hemi under the 1995 Dodge Avenger body of Hodgson's funny car.

ABOVE & LEFT: Ron Hope's "Rat Trap" at full noise is a sight to behold. Since its initial construction in late 1968 and debut in early 1969, no other Fuel Altered has been as highly publicised as the "Rat Trap". Running a Bantam body and Dennis Watson chassis with independent front suspension, this crazy altered boasts a nitro burning Chrysler Hemi built and tuned by Don Green. It was originally campaigned with several different drivers from 1969 to 1973 when it was sold to a new owner in Alaska. The car Ron and his team brought to Sydney is an exact recreation of the original. It was built in 1995/'96 and has been tearing up race tracks accross the world since 1997.

BELOW: As a youngster, Shawn Callen once helped crew on the "High Heaven" altered of Les and Cal Jackson from Denver, Colorado. Several years later, while living in Alaska in the late nineties, Shawn purchased the car as a roller and ran it in Alaska with blown 350 Chevy power, naming the altered "Mighty Mouse". In 2007 Shawn moved and took the altered to Boise, Idaho where it was restored back to its original 1974 "High Heaven" configuration by March 2011. The car runs a 427 tall deck Chevy big block topped with a Littlefield blower and an Enderle "Bug Catcher" injector hat.

ABOVE & RIGHT: "Dangerous" Dave Gould shipped his blown big block Chevy powered fuel altered, "Nightmare" over to Australia from Tauranga, New Zealand and lived up to his nickname with some frighteningly wild driving. Dave is the current New Zealand record holder for AA/FA.

BELOW: Shane Olive launches "Psycho III", a car that was built for cacklefests but ended up racing thanks to a huge resurgence in nostalgia drag racing.

ABOVE: Australian drag racing legend, Graeme Cowin helps stage his "Psycho III" AA Fuel Altered with Shane Olive behind the wheel. Graeme's first altered, spelled, "Phycho" was a Ford powered Fiat Topolino that made its debut in 1967. Graeme and wife, Wendy then built "Psycho II" using a T bucket body and second-hand parts in 1973, and eventually sold it to Bob Shepherd to allow the couple to buy in on a speed shop business, now known as Rocket Industries. Cowin went on to successfully compete in funny car and Top Fuel dragsters during the eighties and nineties and built the current, "Psycho III" to use as a cackle car. In 1993 Cowin became the first driver outside of the USA to run a five second quarter mile pass, in 1995 he was Top Fuel Champion, and in 2018 was inducted into the Australian Motorsport Hall of Fame.

ABOVE & RIGHT: A flame-shooting test run in the pits draws an enthusiastic crowd late in the afternoon. Morice McMillin flew the flag for the Kiwis in the blown Hemi powered, "Spooky" altered and below, beats Rich Guasco's "Pure Hell" off the start line.

ABOVE & RIGHT: Randy and Sue Bradford brought their AA/FA 1938 Fiat Topolino out to Sydney from California. It runs a nitromethane fed, 2800 horsepower, blown 417 Donovan Hemi in a 110 inch chassis and has produced a best quarter mile in 6.055 seconds at 237.60 mph. Randy has been drag racing since 1963 when he ran a '55 Chevy gasser with his father, Brad. The original Fiat Topolino hit US strips in 1966 and won many races across the States until it was retired in the early '70s. This replica was finished in 2000.

BELOW & RIGHT: Rich Guasco's "Pure Hell" is the world's quickest and fastest AA Fuel Altered. The original car first hit the drag strip back in 1964 with small block Chevy power and was the first fuel altered to go over 180 mph and under 8.50 seconds. A Chrysler Hemi was installed in 1968 and reset the speed record at 207 mph with a best ET of 7.27 at 214 mph. In 1969 that car was destroyed in a highway accident and sold. Rich then purchased what was left of the car in 1992 and faithfully restored it, raced it again for a few years and eventually retired "Pure Hell". This replica was built by Davey Uyehara with a 14 inch longer wheelbase, as per Rich's specifications, and built to the 1960s Fuel Altered rules with a true 25% engine set-back and period correct 12 inch M&H tyres. Rich's best times with it then were 6.36 seconds and 238 mph. The car was then retired before returning in 2009 and updated. It's now driven by Brian Hope and runs a Dale Emery billet 392 Hemi. Best times to date are 6.053 seconds at a top speed of 244.74 mph. Brian took the win in round one with a 6.2 second pass against Kiwi, Morice McMillin in "Agro" but a round two transmission/reverser issue ended the day for "Pure Hell".

ABOVE: Peter Byrne in John Gauci's Speed Gas dragster takes on Michael Watkins in a Boosted Outlaws altered matchup.
LEFT: John Somoracz recently built this fuel altered Fiat Topolino and had it on display amongst a great field of cacklefest cars. It runs a blown Hemi topped with a rare, Aussie P/R injector hat from the early seventies.
BELOW: Norm Stewart had his late father, Mark's blown, injected six cylinder Holden powered altered, "Panic 179" on display.

BELOW: Dean Wallan's Fiat Topolino, "The Flying Circus" boasts injected big block Chevy power. Unfortunately we didn't get to hear it run.

ABOVE & RIGHT: Rick Gauci piloted the Aussie "Chucky's Toy" fuel altered, one of Graham Cowin's fleet of altereds and funny cars that make regular appearances at Aussie drag strips.

ABOVE & BELOW: Paul Messineo in "Agro" faces off against Rich Guasco's famous, "Pure Hell" from the USA.

BELOW: Stephen Biggs launches his "Loose Cannon" '56 Chevy against Damien Kemp in the "Funderbolt" gasser.

ABOVE: Steve Costa's "Blaster" big block powered '57 Chevy loves a wheelstand.
ABOVE RIGHT: A pair of black coupes from the Hot Rod bracket smoke it up.
BELOW: A huge field of 34 gassers put on a great show in the Vintage Gas bracket. Here we have New Zealand's, Dave Best in the Model A coupe and Simon Adrichem in the injected big block Chevy powered FX Holden, "Mr Shifter" lifting the front wheels high into the air side by side – awesome! Dave Best built his coupe in the early nineties. It runs an injected 392 Hemi backed by a four speed gearbox.

ABOVE & RIGHT: Chelsea Leahy piloted the "Rocket Ship" while father, Greg Leahy handled the "Nitro Sheriff" wheel-standing funny cars and put on a great show for the crowd.
BELOW: Kiwi, GT Norris' "Pist 'n' Broke" 1953 Kaiser Frazer Henry J gasser runs a 1967 440 Plymouth, 727 Torqeflite and Oldsmobile diff.

ABOVE RIGHT: Craig Mukllan brought his 1959 Studebaker Lark, "Larkness Monster" over from New Zealand. It runs a 350 Chevy backed by a Borg Warner Super T10 four speed and nine inch diff.
RIGHT: Simon Moir warming the tyres of his Willys gasser, "Ruff 'n' Ready".

Story & Pics: Larry O'Toole

LEFT: Don Lokken 1937 Chev ute, Sherwood Park, AB. Slick custom fitting work allows the hard tonneau to fit flush with its surrounds, recessed taillights and licence plate in a rolled pan clean up the rear aspect. Painted running boards add to the updated appearance as do the large diameter billet spoked wheels, flush fitting tailgate and fuel filler in the rear fender.

Coupe utes are a vehicle design unique to Australia, but that doesn't stop them being exported to other places in the world. Here's a selection that was gathered in the USA during 2019 that is representative of the breed in street rod form.

Utes were usually subjected to a rough working life, often as farm vehicles, so their survival rate isn't high. Adding to their rarity is the fact that the Australian motor vehicle market wasn't very large in the 1930s and 1940s.

For the uninitiated the unique design of the Aussie coupe ute lies in its car based body style with a cargo bed that is designed to be integral with the cab section, unlike the separate, usually truck based designs of American pickups from the same era. The result was a comfortable passenger vehicle that could double as a workhorse for the farmer or tradesman.

The somewhat spartan original design of most coupe utes responds well to the full street rod treatment with improvements to the design and mild customising resulting in a slick, personalised ride. like those shown here. ■

RIGHT: Virgil Kuzz 1940 Ford Deluxe ute, Sherwood Park, AB. Virgil's '40 Ford ute is fitted with a flush fitting hard tonneau in similar fashion to Don Lokken's '37 Chevy. The three quarter rear shot really emphasises the near vertical rear of cab roof panel that is unique to utes and differs from coupes. Two tone paintwork gives Virgil's ute an upmarket style that is set off with billet spoke wheels. Once again a flush fitting tailgate and fuel filler door really add to the clean styling.

ABOVE & INSET: Virgil Kuzz's 1940 Ford Ute is a rare model for any ute but more so because this one is a Deluxe model. Many utes were factory built as the Standard model due to their projected life as a work vehicle. Rounded rear fenders are unique to the ute body style.

LEFT & INSET: John Nissen's 1946 Mercury ute is one of only 70 built in 1946 and 215 overall for the three year series, 1946-7-8. Ford saw the market for a more stylish ute and went into production with the longer wheelbase Mercury ute that was sold alongside the more popular regular Ford model.

ABOVE, RIGHT & BELOW: Improvements to the frontal styling of Don Lokken's 1937 Chevy ute include a billet aluminium grille and the bumper mounted closer to the bodywork. The top of the engine hood has also been converted to one piece design whereas the original version featured a centre hinge. Modern rear vision mirrors have been blended into the forward lower corners of the door windows. Don's ute was for sale at the time the photos were taken.

BELOW: Rear view of John Nissen's 1946 Mercury ute shows a smoothed and rolled rear pan and chromed tailgate hinges. Interior trim is finished in bone leather with a '50 Ford dash fitted in place of the original.

LEFT & RIGHT: Oscar Andersen's 1940 Ford Standard ute, from Marysville WA. Compare Oscar's ute with the Deluxe version of the same model shown on the previous pages. Oscar's silver grey version has 4.6 Mustang GT engine, automatic transmission, power windows, air conditioning and heating, plus power seats. The ute was for sale for US$65,000.00 at the time the photos were taken during the Goodguys North West Nationals at Puyallup in 2019. The rear of Oscar's ute retains its original styling, overlapping tailgate and exposed fuel filler. Inside there is grey leather trim with fabric inserts and an engine turned billet dash insert for the aftermarket gauges.

LEFT & BELOW: 1937 Chevy ute, Joe and Val Fort, Nanaimo, BC. Glossy black paint graces the bodywork of Joe and Val's ute that has been updated with many custom features. The hard tonneau is modified Dodge truck that fits flush with the ute's sides and is supported by gas rams. Red leather makes the interior really stand out against the black paint and the trim theme has been carried through to the ute bed. The tailgate has been sealed up and smoothed off with quad exhaust outlets in the rolled rear pan.

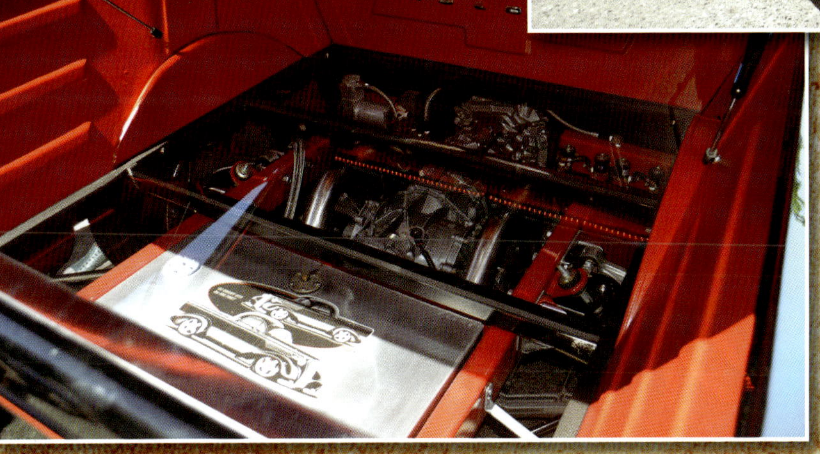

LEFT: All '97 Corvette running gear is used in the Chevy ute including a six speed manual transmission. Fibreglass fenders and running boards are two inches wider than stock with protection strips added to the tops of the running boards. A Lexan floor panel in the bed lets observers see what's underneath, including a stainless steel exhaust sysem and there's a Mazda third brake light built into the back of the tonneau cover. A split front bumper has LED park lights inserted and there's a custom made aluminium gas tank mounted between the rear chassis rails. Highly polished billet aluminium wheels have their own custom "ute" badges in the centres.

Fat Fender Family

Words & Photos: Larry O'Toole

I t is hard to imagine what it is like to have your street rod voted as the top car at a Street Rod Nationals. Few people get to realise that dream and for Mick Speranza it happened at the ASRF Nationals in Bendigo in 2017. His superbly crafted '35 Ford coupe was the stand out car that weekend, but for Mick it was really the culmination of a lifelong desire to build his own hot rods to the best of his ability. There is no doubt about that ability, as attested to by his workshop filled with '35-'36 Fords. Mind you it's not only Mick's doing, this is a family thing for the Speranza's with wife Kim having her own street rod, a perfect '36 Ford roadster.

Of course the Speranza story goes back a long way, in fact all the way to Mick's apprenticeship days as a machinist in a Footscray factory where he worked under a grumpy fully qualified machinist who refused to teach him anything, lest he someday displace the older worker. Not to be denied, Mick put his head down and worked hard to learn his trade without the assistance of the tradesman and did indeed take the top job when things tightened up in the industry. There's no doubt that doggedness has paid huge dividends for Mick, not only in advancing his knowledge and prowess with machines, but also to be able to stick to a task and see it through to the end. We all know that's a major factor in building a street rod, let alone several of them! Mick no longer works as a machinist, but there is no doubt that trade background has served him well in his chosen hobby.

Mick now owns the '36 Ford roadster used to make the mould for the fibreglass Deuce Customs bodies that came from WA, where it had been owned and stored for many years by Neville Marney. It is a mint original with not a sign of rust anywhere, a real bonus that will see it turned into another classy street rod at Mick's hands. Not another contemporary street rod this time though, Mick is already well into the build and is going with a '60s period style theme on the roadster. The beam axle front end is being retained, along with the transverse sprung early rear end, hotted up flathead engine, that formerly resided in a HAMB racer, and wide five '39 Ford wheels with polished spider caps. It's going to be another beauty.

But we are getting ahead of ourselves, time to go back and pick up the story line before we became distracted by the roadster.

There have been several other projects Mick has completed over the years and he has collected several more as running vehicles and then added his own touch to them. The collection is indeed impressive, especially if you are a '35-'36 Ford fan.

However we will start right at the beginning when Mick was only 18 years of age. That's when he stripped and rebuilt his first car. Mick grew up watching American Graffiti and Happy Days so he always had hot rodding in the back of his mind.

He bought a '34 Chev coupe from Ballan and got to know a few other guys with '34 Chevs.

The family moved from Sunshine to Deer Park when Mick was 11 years old. He got to know a guy with Chevs who took him to meet Duncan McFarlane and Tony Wilkins, both of whom were Chev guys who had the kind of cars he liked. At that stage, Mick was into Chevs and that was it, he knew nothing about Fords.

He soon found out that Chevs of this era were full of wood, so he started looking for cars that were less work. The search resulted in the purchase of a '35 Ford coupe that Mick bought as a registered and running car, but it needed lots of work. He set about chopping the roof and put in a blown 350 Chevy engine, nine inch diff etc. It was the first real hot rod that Mick built, but he also bought others; typical was a '36 Ford coupe that was half done, completed and sold again. Next was a '34 Ford roadster that was also purchased as a finished car. It was an old Drag-Ens car from Sydney to which he added a new bonnet, new paint and whitewall tyres. This car Mick drove for awhile, but he always wanted a '35 Ford three window coupe, so he started looking.

It wasn't long before one turned up on American eBay, for sale in Colorado. Mick bought it sight unseen and a friend imported it for him. This is the black coupe that was voted Top Street Rod at the 2017 ASRF Street Rod Nationals. The original purchase was Mick's 40th birthday present to himself.

In 2008, before the black three window coupe was built, Mick built a roadster for Kim. She had seen Al Borserio's '36 Ford roadster and liked it, so they built their own version. The roadster is built on an original chassis by Mick and uses a Deuce Customs fibreglass repro body. They already had the metal front clip, so that went on the front of the roadster and Mick did all the bodywork, but had it painted by a friend. Mick also built the roof

frame himself and then had it trimmed by an upholsterer.

Mick previously owned a '32 Ford roadster as well. Con Mantzaris came to do the SR plate permit check for the '32 roadster, saw the '36 chassis and body and asked, "When will you finish this?"

"It will be ready for Bright," was the answer.

That was only seven months away and Con's response was, "You will never get it done in seven months."

Kim's roadster was finished two days before Bright and had only done a 25 kilometre test drive before she set off for Bright, confidently informing Mick, "You built it for me, so I am driving it!"

Well it won a Top Ten trophy on that first outing; icing on the cake after such a frantic build.

With the roadster out of the way, Mick started from scratch on the '35 Ford three window coupe that was stripped and bare metal prepped. Greg Jones built the chassis and master metal crafter, Andy Scicluna helped with the top chop. All of the remainder of the bodywork was done by Mick in high fill and then it was handed over to CAD Customs who painted it glossy black. Essentially, Mick built the car around the Halibrand Quick-Change and the wheels. It was entered in MotorEx and Mick was still bolting bits on the morning it went to the show.

"I hadn't seen it as a completed car and it turned out exactly as I hoped". The coupe was built for me, trophies weren't a consideration, but hot rodders gave it the best trophy of all when they voted it Top Street Rod at the Nationals.

After MotorEx, Mick drove it quite a bit then entered the Victorian Hot Rod Show. No trophies resulted but prominent local hot rodder, Rod Hadfield made Mick's day when he told him, "This was the best car in the show!" Better than a trophy! The coupe had been on the road for three years prior to the 2017 Nationals, going to runs like Queenscliff but not too far away from home. Mick and Kim took both cars to Bendigo for the Nationals, enjoyed the weekend and come presentations Mick thought, "It

Caribbean Stud
NO ENTRY

would be nice to get a Top 20 trophy." But they got to 19 and he thought he had missed out. Still he had a great weekend and then it got even better when the Top Street Rod announcement was made and out came Mick's name. "I went into a daze, I didn't know what was happening, everyone was happy for me and offering congratulations – it was an absolute blast".

Soon after, the couple jumped in the roadster went for a drive, people going past recognised us and made us feel like celebrities. The smiles lasted for the next six months because it wasn't expected.

Mick and Kim are now amazed at how many people know your car. Interstaters were saying they had been waiting to see this car.

"You don't realise the impact you can have on people."

Mick went to the USA in 2013, looking for a roadster, but only saw one at Hollywood Hot Rods that was not for sale, it was there to be built as a project for its owner. On return Mick asked a friend to keep a look out for one for him. Within a week he told me there was one coming up for sale in Western Australia, the one used for the Deuce Customs mould. Again Mick bought a car sight unseen, it was still in bits after being used for mould. This car is now his next project that he hopes to have finished in two years.

There are more early Fords in the Speranza collection. The blue '36 Ford three window coupe just popped up for sale. Mick knew about the car from its previous history – ex California, it had been for sale on American eBay with a reserve of $60,000.00 after which it seemed to disappear. California hot rod builder, Alex Guzzardi apparently built the car after which it went to New Zealand. The new owner wasn't happy with it even after rebuilding the chassis, suspension and engine so he sold it to a mate who then moved to Queensland in Australia. A friend of Mick's saw the coupe at a Wintersun run, asked if it was for sale and swapped details. The owner didn't want to sell then, but called six months later to sell it so he could start a new business. Mick's friend couldn't afford it so he rang Mick and he instantly recognised the car. Mick didn't hesitate, he knew he was going to buy it before he even saw it. The deposit was paid and the coupe came to live with Mick and Kim. The satin black three window coupe was advertised in NSW for a while, causing Mick to think, "Wouldn't it be good to have two three windows. The owner already had a small block Chevy in it, but was asking top money. Mick had a '75 Camaro that he was driving too hard and realised he would lose his licence if he kept it. He rang the guy to see if he would trade with cash adjustment. The coupe owner agreed, they met at Holbrook and did the deal

on the spot, each driving the other car home. Mick soon found the coupe needed some work, but it was quickly sorted out. Now he uses it as almost a daily driver, towing his caravan etc. It has a 327 engine, Muncie four speed and is a real good body without any patch panels in it. One day Mick intends to rebuild it as a tail dragger.

Having just bought the satin black three window coupe, Mick then found himself in possession of a '41 Lincoln Coupe that he bought the same week.

"I never thought I would find one, but Kim found it when talking to a guy at a panel shop." He showed her some of the cars he owned and after he left Kim told Mick he had three Lincoln Zephyrs. Mick's response was, "I only want one!" The Lincoln owner had wanted to buy Mick's '35 three window coupe when he saw it being painted. When Kim told him about the Lincoln he asked to be considered if it ever came up for sale. In due course there was a phone call, "He's thinking about getting rid of one." But he didn't want to sell it to just anyone, offered it to three guys, two in Victoria and one in South Australia. The instructions were, if they were interested just make an offer. Mick realised he had to make an offer, but how much? Only one of the others put in an offer, so Mick offered what he thought was a fair price and the owner, although hoping for a bit more, agreed, knowing it was going to a good home. He rang at 10:00am and the Lincoln coupe was in Mick's shed by 2:00pm, allowing no time for the seller to change his mind. The other interested buyer was devastated.

"Every time I drive the Lincoln it blows me away," says Mick. It has a flathead Ford V8, replacing the original V12 long before it came to Australia. The last registration was in Michigan in 1998. After getting the coupe home it only took about $1000.00 to get it going. Mick poured some fuel down the carby and it ran! He drove up and down the driveway, put in a new fuel tank, re-sleeved the master and wheel cylinders and put it on the H plate Club Permit scheme. He's been driving it ever since. The previous owner has been for a drive, happy it went to a good home. The coupe has a three speed manual transmission with overdrive behind the flathead V8 and it does everything it should with style and grace.

Mick and Kim have been married for 27 years and consider hot rodding as a family thing. Children Danielle, Kaitlyn and Georgia are grown up now but all spent their childhood going to rod runs. They do remember it all, probably hated it at the time, but now realise how good it was for their general knowledge and activity. They all loved going to Bright and Queenscliff, would still love to go, but mostly work commitments mean they seldom get the chance. The girls don't claim to be hot rodders, but they know what hot rodding is all about.

Time now to talk about the original '36 Ford roadster. After settling it in his workshop, Mick bought a HAMBster dragster with a worked 8BA Ford sidevalve engine that will be going into the '36 roadster. It will be built in '60s period style with triple carbs and Edelbrock heads on the engine. Mick has been collecting rare stuff for the roadster, including a very rare set of bonnet feathers that he had been after for years. They came up just before Christmas 2018 for big dollars but Mick just had to have them. He will keep the HAMBster and put another sidevalve in it for some fun at the Nostalgia Drags.

At the Bendigo National Swap Meet Mick bought some aftermarket spider caps to suit '36 Fords that retain their wide five wheel bolt pattern. He had been chasing a set of these for a long time and found them at this swap meet. He was walking towards some shiny things that were drawing me to them like a magnet. He was thinking, "It can't be, but there they are!" This rare find made Mick so happy the rest of the swap meet meant nothing to him. Early Ford guru, Ernie Ford told Mick, "You could look for another 20 years and never find another set like that!" Mick now has everything else for the car and the project is under way.

There's another project already planned for once the roadster is completed too. This one will be a '35 Ford sedan delivery that will become the swap meet parts chaser. Mick already has the vehicle, he just needs to get it out of storage. "I have my dream car '35 three window coupe – my heart and soul went into that car, I bought everything the best I could find for that car.

Recently a new old stock '35 grille landed in Mick's hands that is too good to put on a car! This example is absolutely perfect and complete with all of its original polished trims – a life treasure that can stay on the wall, since Mick likes it so much. Mick found a way to purchase the grille by selling other parts to make it affordable.

Mick has no plans after the '35 sedan delivery but would like to spend a bit more time driving and less time in the shed. He and Kim want to enjoy the cars while they can. Somehow I doubt the delivery will be Mick's last project, he loves building them too much!

Deuce Days
2019
New Zealand
1932
Words and Photos: Larry O'Toole
32PHTN

ABOVE: That's a big block Chevy engine riding under the lengthened half hood on Grant Blackwood's Wellington based Tudor. Note the slimline grille shell and chromed Rallye wheels.

Deuce Days New Zealand was staged in Masterton, situated in the lower southeast corner of the North Island. The event was based at the Copthorne Hotel Resort, an eminently suitable venue where most of the entrants stayed, giving Deuce Days an intimate nature. Registration was held at Magoo's Street Rods where owner and event organiser, Lloyd Wilson played host.

Once registered, entrants were offered a choice of things to see to fill in the remainder of the afternoon before the evening welcome and dinner back at the Copthorne Resort. We took the opportunity to visit The Pointon Collection, owned by Francis and Gaye Pointon based just out of Masterton. The collection includes 30 plus vintage and veteran cars along with motorcycles and an extensive collection of period clothing to the mid 1960s. Their collection policy is based on the fact that the item needed to have a connection to the town, the region or New Zealand.

Back at the hotel entrants boarded a bus and were taken to the local movie theatre (built in 1931 so almost exactly the right era), supplied with ice cream and popcorn, and watched a 1932 Ford promotional black and white clip on the big screen, followed by the Deuce of Spades movie.

On return to the hotel, the Friday evening dinner and welcome was enjoyed by all the participants with a delicious buffet meal served by the resort staff.

Saturday morning, more than 60 Deuces lined up for a tour of the region, starting with a visit to Magoo's own "Man Cave", where they drooled over the vast collection of cars and memorabillia. The cruise continued through the nearby countryside to visit the Wildlife

ABOVE: Registration for the Deuce Days Run took place at Magoo's Street Rods premises on the Friday where this bunch gathered for a news photo for the local newspaper. In the foreground is the red, chopped three window coupe of Tony Headland from Southside Streeters.

ABOVE: Left to right we have Jon Oldridge's blue hiboy roadster from Eastside Street Rods, Paul de Martin's neat as a pin, closed cab pickup and the restored five window coupe of Clive Taylor. The light blue hiboy roadster at far right is owned by Americars member Richard Quaid.

LEFT: Nothing looks better than a high quality line up of black '32 Fords. Front to back they are the hiboy roadster of Grant Longley (winner of Best Hiboy Roadster), a near duplicate minus hood sides owned by Alan Hulse of Southside Streeters and at the far end the full fendered Tudor owned by Steve Sharpe of East Bay Rods.

Sanctuary at Mt Bruce. Here they saw some of the endangered species and witnessed eels being fed, as well as being able to walk through the forest of ferns and lush undergrowth. Altogether, a very relaxing experience.

The remainder of the day was free for entrants to relax and check out some of the local attractions. The dinner that evening was again back at the Copthorne Resort where everyone mixed well, caught up with old friends, or made new acquaintances.

Different to most events like this, the prize giving was done in conjunction with breakfast on the Sunday morning as the entry cost included admission to the last day of the New Zealand Drag Racing Nationals at the Masterton Motorplex. Celebrity guest from USA, Troy Ladd spoke about his business Hollywood Hot Rods and I was invited to talk a little about my own life in hot rodding. Awards were presented for Troy's pick of each of the various Deuce body styles. On arrival at the drag strip, the Deuces got to do a parade lap in front of the spectators during a break in racing and then parked up in their own separate area adjacent to the spectator stands. Those needing to travel some distance to get home before nightfall could then leave whenever it suited them, while those living closer to Masterton were able to stay on and enjoy the racing.

Deuce Days New Zealand was again a great success and organiser, Lloyd Wilson indicated it would probably happen again in 2022 to coincide with the 90th anniversary of the Deuce. ■

Deuce Days

ABOVE: Plenty of attitude in these two Deuces. The copper Tudor with Y block Ford power is Craig Stare's beauty, while the blown Hemi powered yellow three window coupe belongs to Ian Vibert.

BELOW: All of the Deuces looked magnificent parked together during the visit to Lloyd Wilson's home property, where the entrants got to check out Magoo's private collection at close quarters.

ABOVE: The group at Magoo's private property from a different angle with Lloyd's own flathead Ford powered, grey three window in the left foreground.

TOP LEFT: Mark Wilkins' blue three window coupe is a perfect rendition of this style of street rod, complete with Chrysler Hemi engine, American five spoke wheels and stock, full fendered body. It was voted Top Fendered Three Window Coupe.

TOP RIGHT: Equally as perfect an example of the hiboy roadster style is the Rodder's Choice winning roadster of Bert Dove from the Oceanside club. Berts roadster is powered by a perfectly dressed and souped up flathead V8 engine.

ABOVE LEFT: You'll need your sunglasses to view Lyall and Lucy Stewart's candy red three window coupe when the sun comes out. The bright chopped beauty is blown small block Chevy powered.

ABOVE RIGHT: Stock bodied but hiboy style three window coupe has dressed flathead engine topped with twin Stromberg 97s and vintage style air cleaners. Owner is Brian Kilsby from Tararua Rodders, winner of Best Hiboy Three Window Coupe.

LEFT: Red wire wheels and dark blue paint are perfect for Sandy Wadsworth's closed cab pickup. Note that Sandy's pickup retains its original style commercial grille along with painted headlight bar, headlight bodies and ah-ooga style horn.

ABOVE: This line up at the Mt Bruce National Wildlife Reserve is headed by the stock, original roadster of Jim Goulding that was hastily assembled for the run. Next in line is Bruce Wadsworth's blue, hiboy five window coupe.

ABOVE: Lance Topliss, from the West Coast Roadents owns this tidy, silver hiboy roadster with Wanlass windshield and five spoke wheels.

MAIN: Lloyd "Magoo" Wilson was chief organiser of the event and is shown here leading a group on the Saturday morning run.

BELOW: Separate parking at the Masterton Motorplex drag strip allowed entrants to take in the National Drags. The green, Chevy powered five window coupe belongs to Nick Seed and Maureen Blanchard from Christchurch.

TOP LEFT: At the Mt Bruce National Wildlife Reserve, this stock original three window coupe called in to mix with the flash versions. It is owned by Grahame Cottle and has been in his family since new!

ABOVE LEFT: We don't often see Deuce Sport Coupes anywhere these days so Len Wilsher's orange example attracted a lot of attention.

LEFT: Stray Katz Cruizers member, Ian Jones brought along his hiboy roadster that sports painted wheels and black cloth top. Kiwi rodders can run fenderless with an exemption, so there were plenty of that style of street rod in attendance.

TOP: A couple of stylised phantom bodied Deuces that make use of Osborne fibreglass repro bodies. On the left is the cabriolet of Les Chesham while the roadster pickup version was entered by Ron Gubb.

RIGHT: How's this for attitude and stance? On the bridge is the hiboy roadster of Greg Hurndell followed by Jon Oldridge's similar styled version.

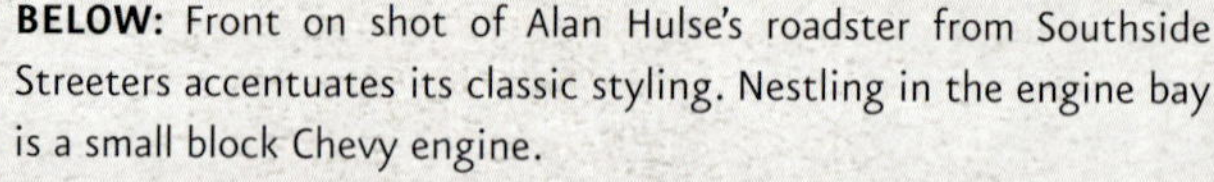

BELOW: Something you don't see every day is a pair of Deuces with big block Chevy W engines. The white three window in the foreground is owned by Darren Dye, while Len Wilsher's Sport Coupe rests in the background.

BELOW: Front on shot of Alan Hulse's roadster from Southside Streeters accentuates its classic styling. Nestling in the engine bay is a small block Chevy engine.

RIGHT: Tim Williams' green hiboy roadster and Tony Headland's red three window coupe prepare to leave the host hotel complex.

BELOW: This one means business. The whole Harris family are into high performance and Lincoln's hiboy roadster certainly exudes that style in abundance. Under that hood scoop resides a healthy blown big block Chevy engine.

ABOVE RIGHT: Flathead fans will warm to this example in Murray Helm's orange three window hiboy coupe. It's equipped with triple Holley 94s and Offenhauser finned heads.

ABOVE: Rear shot of the trophy winning hiboy roadster of Jon Oldridge should get your hiboy juices flowing. In front is the fully fendered five window coupe of Paul Emery, another trophy winner that took out Best Fendered Five Window Coupe.

TOP: What better way to spend the Sunday of Deuce Days than watching the National Drags at Masterton Motorplex against the backdrop of the cloud tipped mountains in the distance?

MAIN: If you like hiboy roadsters, you are probably fairly taken by this rear shot of Gordon Cochrane's bright red example, with big quick-change rear end peeking out from under the rear and those meaty rear tyres on American five spoke wheels. The swoopy look is enhanced even more with the use of a slanted windshield, bobbed rear rails and custom rear pan where the fuel tank normally resides.

TOP: On arrival at the Masterton Motorplex, the Deuces were paraded up and down the strip during a break in the racing and then made their way to a special parking area adjacent to the main spectator bleachers.
BELOW: Check out the height difference between Clive Taylor's stock five window coupe that was driven by special guest Troy Ladd from Hollywood Hot Rods for the weekend and the low riding hiboy roadster of Richard Quaid.

BELOW: Basking in the bright sunshine on the forecourt of their motel are the three roadsters of Tom Gloy from Nevada, John Leonti from California and Sid Chavers from California, each displaying its own individual styling as applied to the same basic car.

There is nothing quite like Deuce Days North West. Can you imagine shutting down the entire centre of a major city for a rod run show and shine at the peak of the holiday season in one of the most popular tourist destinations in North America. That's what they do in Victoria, Vancouver Island when the Deuce Days event comes to the island every three years. Last held in 2016, the 2019 Deuce Days event followed much the same theme as previous versions with entrants enjoying a Poker Run on the Saturday, a dinner in the Victoria Conference Centre on Saturday evening and then the big attraction, the show in the central city streets of Victoria on the Sunday.

Victoria must be one of the most picturesque cities in the world being snuggled around the end of an inlet from the Pacific Ocean that is home to all sorts and sizes of water craft and overseen by the magnificent Fairmont Empress Hotel right on the end of the inlet. Adjacent is the equally majestic Legislature building and several other prominent early examples of 19th century architecture and you have almost the perfect backdrop for 1400 street rods, shining in perfect mid-summer weather, warm but not hot. It was in the streets that serve and

ABOVE: A total pale green colour scheme really suits Larry Leffler's hiboy roadster that also sports large louvres in the hood top.
BELOW: Not a Ford but still a '32, this coupe is a Buick owned by Ron and Roberta Latham and powered by a Cadillac V8.

ABOVE: Black painted artillery style wheels and low set commercial headlights are just a couple of the features of Rick Bales' black hiboy.
BELOW: More black artillery style wheels adorn this blue, full fendered roadster entered by David Lyon of Portland, Oregon.

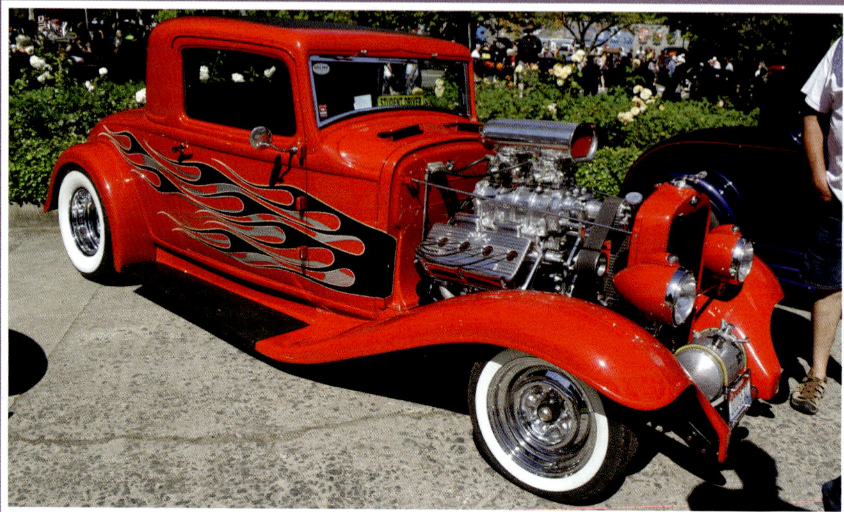

ABOVE: Brown Tudor with black fenders provides a nice contrast to all the roadsters. This one is owned by John Lawson.

BELOW: Flathead power for Gordon Gray's slant windshield equipped hiboy roadster that has Cragar spinners on black painted wheels and dirt track tyres.

BELOW: Another non-Ford '32, this time the red with flames Dodge from Sandpoint, Idaho with blown 392 Hemi engine. Note the dual cowl vents and longer than usual Guide style lights.

surround this magnificent centre that the cars of Deuce Days were assembled on July 22 for their day in the sun. Setting up for the show and shine began at 3:30am and by daylight all was in readiness for the thousands of visitors to pour through the best car show in the world.

Over 100,000 people, according to official estimates, came to the show on the Sunday resulting in every inch of the show areas being crowded with happy smiling people. Jostling for photos was hard work, but rewarding, as you can see right here on these pages.

Organisers tried hard to ensure all the Deuces were parked together near the centre and succeeded for the most part, but when you have 650 of them, plus another 750 non-Deuce entries to fit in the allocated spaces, you can imagine the logistics of pulling that off. It only took a committee of 90 people (yes 90!), but they did it with aplomb under the expert co-ordinating skills of chief organiser Al Clark.

Entrants came from all over North America for Deuce Days, such is the pulling power of this event, indeed this year there was even an entry that came all the way from New Zealand.

Will there ever be another one? Time will tell, but if there is, consider adding it to your bucket list, you won't regret it.

RIGHT: Candy red paint and an injected small block Ford engine make Lorne Embree's roadster stand out in the crowd.

ABOVE: It's hard to imagine a more suitable setting for a car show than the streets of downtown Victoria. The stately Empress Hotel dominates the background and the Deuces dominate the foreground, none more so than Nick Testa's delightful blue hiboy roadster.

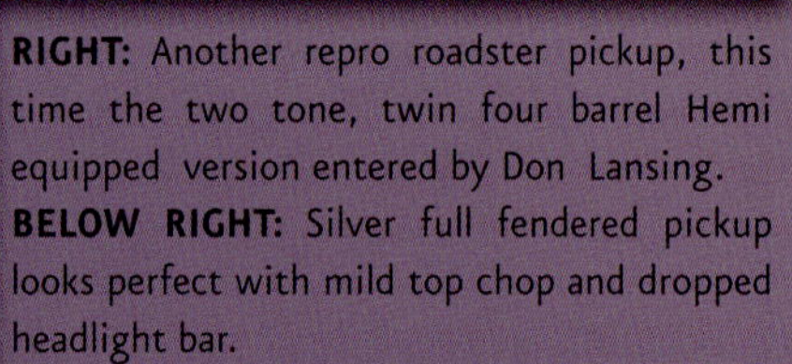

RIGHT: Another repro roadster pickup, this time the two tone, twin four barrel Hemi equipped version entered by Don Lansing.
BELOW RIGHT: Silver full fendered pickup looks perfect with mild top chop and dropped headlight bar.

ABOVE: Lots of nostalgic touches on Jim's hiboy roadster including early style Halibrand solid magnesium wheels and a blown all-alloy Don Ferguson built Ardun in the engine bay.

ABOVE: Sitting in pride of place for the Sunday show is the "So Low" scalloped hiboy roadster of event organiser Al Clark, a local resident of Victoria who did a marvelous job of organising the whole event.

TOP LEFT: Lines of Deuces like this were on display everywhere you looked. At the head of this bunch is the black and scalloped roadster owned by Troy Adams.
ABOVE: Repeat that description as we look across a predominantly blue line of '32 hoods. In the foreground is the rare sedan delivery of William Johnson.

LEFT: Peeking out from the engine bay of Chick Koszis' roadster is a potent Hemi engine with lakes style headers. Commercial headlights with a chromed tie-bar add a touch of class to the frontal appearance.

BELOW: Tidy closed cab pickup is actually a '34 Ford, recognisable by the extra body mould line across the rear of the cabin and slightly slanted grille. Otherwise they are very similar to '32 Ford pickups. Another way to pick the difference is to check the engine bay – '32 models used the same separate firewall as the passenger cars.

ABOVE: Gold highlight graphic striping sets this black Tudor apart. Nerf bars and Chevy taillights point to a '60s era heritage. Owner is Keith Bush.

RIGHT: There's always a Graffiti coupe clone when there is a large gathering of Deuces but this one looks very much like the real thing. It was entered by David McCoury from Spokane, Washington.

BELOW: Time for a photo opportunity to show the folks back home what a wonderul time the members of the Over The Hill Gang had in Victoria.

RIGHT: How about some flamed Deuces? Here's a couple of the best in the form of Ted Johnson's magenta graced roadster and Don Hawker's more traditional style version with yellow blending to red flames.

BELOW: Maybe you prefer the red and blue combination on Paul Hoiland's five window coupe with triple carb equipped small block Chevy engine from Kelowna, BC.

BELOW RIGHT: Metallic dark silver full fendered three window coupe has black painted wheels to provide a contrast and low stance to catch your eye, Owner is Rod Wilkinson of Puyallup, Washington.

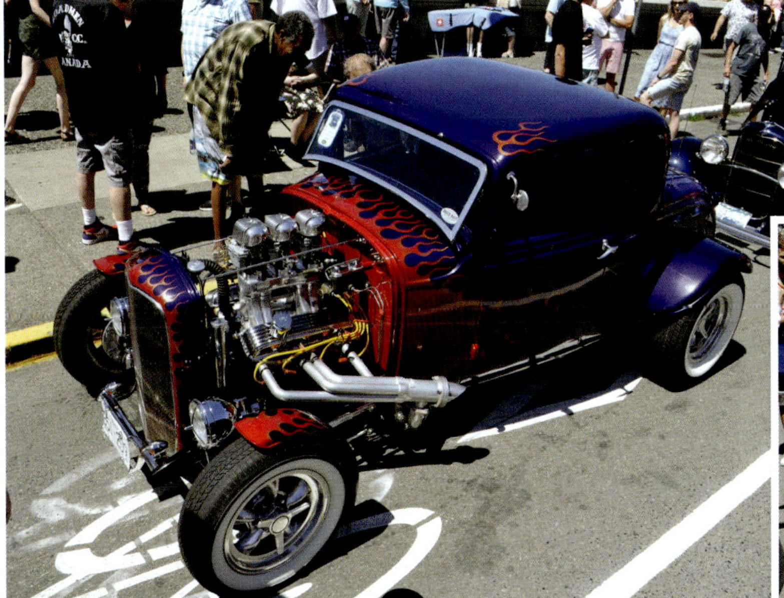

LEFT: Size matters! This beauty is a rare '32 Lincoln Victoria owned by Larry Carter of Los Gatos, California that attracted a constant crowd of admirers. It was suitably parked out the front of the Empress Hotel.

BELOW LEFT: Hiboy sedans are suddenly in vogue and this one with cream wire wheels indicates why. When given the right treatment they look just as good as any of the sportier Deuces.

BELOW: Independent front suspension and bright red paint feature on this three window hiboy coupe owned by Frank Coppinger.

RIGHT: Pretty as a picture is this blue Deuce Victoria with Olds Rocket engine and whitewall tyres on steel wheels.

BELOW RIGHT: We don't see enough channelled Deuces any more but they sure do look good when given the treatment like this one owned by Mike McGowan.

ABOVE: Queen Victoria looks down with approval on these Deuces headed up by Don Lindfors' orange, Ford powered roadster.

ABOVE: There were lots of superb non-Deuce rods on display too. This red '40 Ford coupe was typical of the support show participants.

BELOW RIGHT: There weren't many beater style Deuces on display but this one owned by Pat Swanson of Spokane, Washington was one of the better examples.

BELOW: All the way from Wellington, New Zealand were long distance winners Mark and Robyn Wilkin in their Hemi powered three window coupe.

ABOVE: Mild custom, slant chopped two tone '39 Plymouth sedan delivery with custom shaped DeSoto bumpers exudes class from end to end.

ABOVE: Outstanding Fordor sedan of Don Sangster was chosen as the Participants Choice winner for 2019. Take a minute to absorb some of the refined work on this superb street rod that ticks all the right boxes.

LEFT: At first glance you might not realise this two tone Tudor is actually a '30 Model A with extended engine bay, a healthy big block Ford V8 up front and flip up roof panels.
BELOW: Well executed flames grace the front of this classy '35 Ford three window coupe that has a mild top chop and perfect stance.

LEFT & BELOW: Clean and dropped '40 Ford pickup of Bud Wolfe has painted artillery style wheels and injected small block Ford engine dressed up to look like a Y block.

BELOW LEFT: This one caused some double-takes. It's a modified '56 MGA sports car that has been treated to a Lincoln V12 flathead engine swap.

BOTOM: Low-profile '30 Model A Tudor is chopped and channelled with triple carb equipped flathead V8 running gear and a shortened '34 Chevy grille with custom insert. John Nehuing brought it along to Deuce Days North West.

Striptcaser
LINCOLN V12
Striptcaser

HOP-ON HOP-OFF

ABOVE: Elegant convertible is a '40 Pontiac dressed in sky blue with dark blue leather interior trim. Owner is Stephen Ball.

ABOVE RIGHT: Gary Rubottom's '35 Chevy coupe sits comfortably amongst the other non-Ford cars on display at Deuce Days.

RIGHT: Tall, skinny, black steel wheels and black paint all over identify Jason Rinaldi's Buick Nailhead powered closed cab pickup from Prince Albert, Ontario.

BELOW: There was lots of admiration for Ken Helm's antique racer that features an interesting combination of Mclaughlin and Buick parts.

BOTTOM: Diamond T truck has a new life as a smart looking pickup.

ABOVE: It's hard to comprehend just how much has been changed on Mark Mariani's fully custom built '28 Model A Ford Tudor. It was difficult to photograph because of the large crowd it attracted.

A garage find comes back to life!

Chris and Charis Trombetta
1933 Ford 5 Window Coupe
Seminole, Florida USA

Every hot rod project has a background story, so too do the hot rodders themselves. Chris Trombetta is typical, he owned lots of '55, '56, '57 Chevys, a '33 Ford salt flats racer and a '70 Boss 429 Ford Mustang, one of only 499 made by the Ford factory. With a background like that there is always another project in the wings, in this case another '33 Ford coupe that Chris purchased in 2016. Not just any ordinary garage find '33 coupe, as Chris describes it, this one has a really interesting history.

"A couple of guys were hanging out at the local hot rod shop, NBS Performance in Pinellas Park, Florida USA, home to many well-built, highly modified, fast, street and drag cars. Brothers Dave and Andrew Stephens are the owners. NBS(no bullshit). Like all shops, there is always a mix of old guys and young guys hanging around bench racing; I'm almost old but fit somewhere in between old and young.

One day sitting around I said, 'Hey guys I would like to build an all steel '33-'34 Ford hot rod in the next two years, keep our eyes out for one. Okay! No Rush!' Everyone agreed in an uninterested way, but really had no idea where to find one.

All was quiet for only a few weeks, but when I arrived at NBS as usual on a Saturday, an older hot rod guy, the father figure of the shop, who I

Photos: Al O'Toole
Words: Larry O'Toole

knew very well, cornered me immediately and said he knew where there was a full fendered '33 all steel Ford coupe. Don W had a friend in high school that owned a very fast '33 Ford street racer. It cruised around St Pete, Florida when times were simpler. They used to race for fun and chase girls when they were young and full of energy. Many good times were had in that '33 Ford. In 1962 the owner, Don A was financially able to go to the local Chevy dealership and buy a brand new Corvette 327 replacement engine, the largest, fastest, most powerful, small block Chevy you could purchase, and a Chevy Bowtie embossed T-10 four speed manual transmission. That was the first year of the 327 engine. He installed a cross ram intake manifold with 2x4 carbs, magneto and a 5:13:1 rear gear. That was quite a performance package for 1962 in a light coupe. Don A, the owner, even used Ford stickers on the valve covers to trick many opponents. Many races were won and many axles twisted throughout the years. I have that complete Corvette motor and T-10 now, although not used in the car at the present time.

The car was retired in favor of a Chevy II in January 1966 and placed inside the family's one car garage. That's where we thought we could find it. It was covered in garage stuff over the years and forgotten about, but

still loved very much. My enquiry sparked an interest in reviving the old coupe and the interview process started. No negotiation was entered into until my intentions were clear and there was no wiggle room on the purchase price. Face to face meetings proceeded and a deal was made. The clean out process started at the beginning of 2016. Could it really be 50 years sitting in that garage? Yes, almost to the month. When that coupe was pulled out into the driveway and the light of day shone on it, four senior citizens, friends since high school, were transported in time. Hugs and tears were in order. The coupe was still in quite good condition, even with its original '60s style interior trim intact. What a great day! Pushing it to the trailer with flat tires – not so great!"

The car was sent to NBS Performance, gobs of planning undertaken and some parts sourced. The car required some metal work and a new firewall. It was stripped, separated from the frame, and blasted. Then NBS went to work setting up the initial suspension, updating the ride components, and installing split wishbones with Super Bell dropped axle, building canted ladder bars for the rear and refitting some body panels.

A new motor combination was commissioned from Kris Nelson at Nelson Competition in St Pete, Florida. It came in the form of an all-

Sixties Racer Reborn
FORD

aluminum 421 cubic inch Brodix Chevy street motor with Weber carbs, Zips high-rise water pump to help conceal a low mount air conditioner pump and alternator brackets. Also added to the engine were, a remote oil filter, MSD ignition and a Walker radiator. Headers and full exhaust were custom built to include electric cut-outs.

The transmission is a five speed Tremec manual that transfers the torque via a custom aluminium driveshaft to the Winters V8 quick-change rear end made to a custom width with #3 gear set and a transverse buggy spring for suspension.

"Earlier the year before, I met Chad Adams in Florida where Chad had two '32 Fords on display. We hit it off and the switch was made for Adams Hot Rod Shop to carry the torch and finish the car."

The project was delivered to Chad in October 2017 with a full set of instructions and a boatload of flexibility to allow him to do what he knows best. Over the next year Chad and the Adams Team tore the car apart again and tweaked every component. They notched the front and rear of the chassis, fitted a Vega style steering box, bobbed the rear of the

Sixties Racer Reborn

frame and added a Boling Brothers brake kit with vented backing plates. Chad's team also did all of the bodywork, made every jamb perfect and fixed all the old metal seams.

The roof already sported what seemed to be about a four inch top chop from the late '50s. It looked perfect, so we left it that way. Chad literally addressed every other aspect of the car with a custom touch, most of which you can't readily notice. He also installed a complete interior wood kit from Brad's Woodworking out of Washington State. Suicide door locks were fitted in place, along with swinging pedals mounted into a 90 degree bracket placing the master cylinder under the dash where it shares the space with an under-dash air conditioner with hidden controls and vents.

The coupe is all Ford steel except for the roof filler panel and hood tops. All original parts that could be saved were cleaned, modified and chromed where appropriate. A custom recessed firewall is used that retains all the original markings.

"There were also some special items included. I always wanted a traditional style car, not a modern street rod. Chad's team knew exactly how to do that. They used tons of louvers on the hood, roof insert and trunk lid, all punched by Steve at Total Restoration. Chad split the trunk and made a removable panel so you could clean underneath the outside layer of the trunk. He also fabricated an un-welded roof insert with louvers that is sealed to the interior and has drains in case the car gets caught in the rain."

The front and rear spreader bars were hand built to compliment the curves of the '33 coupe, the underside is all perfect and painted to match the body, while Steel Ford and Wheel Vintique wheels fitted with 5.50R16 front tyres and 7.50R16 Excelsior rear tyres keep the style of the car in context.

Inside there is black leather trim with fabric inserts that feature silver flake and thread over the original front seat, all finished in-house by Adams Hot Rod Shop.

Daytona style black carpet lines the floor and the dash holds all Stewart Warner restored "wings" gauges by Chris Schlaff, including a 150mph police speedometer. All the electrical wiring was carried out by Adams Hot Rod Shop, and connects up 682C Guide headlights and '37 Ford taillights that were modified by the Adams crew as well.

The motor was left all natural aluminium as well as the quick-change rear cover. Everything is either raw aluminium, black or chrome, that's it!

"Chad was great to work with and listened to every comment I had to offer. The car was supposed to be grey, but we changed it to an unreal black a week before it hit the booth. Between NBS discovering this car and starting the process and then the magic touch of Adams Hot Rod Shop this car is unreal! One of the coolest things about the '33 was everyone used to say they could see the instrument lights from the overhead gauges while cruising around town, so we left two gauges in the header panel – for old time's sake!

I do want to commend all the guys from Adams Hot Rod Shop, I truly believe the more they worked on this car, and the more they learned about it, the more they loved it. Special and sincere thanks to Don W for finding the car and Don A for selling the car after 50 years sitting in his garage. Thanks also to NBS Performance and Fabrication for starting the rebuild and laying out the basics and the Adams Hot Rod Shop team for building one hell of a hot rod. Of course my wife Charis gets special credit for putting up with me."

The coupe was finished just in time for the NSRA Street Rod Nationals 50th anniversary in Louisville, Kentucky where it was exhibited in the Builders Showcase. ◼

Bonneville
Speed Week
2019

ABOVE: The Speed Demon team tried hard in adverse conditions and did manage to go home with the Hot Rod magazine trophy for the fastest timed mile at Speed Week.

Anticipation was high for another great Speed Week after the huge success of the 2018 event when racing conditions were the best seen for years. The lead up to 2019 Speed Week wasn't quite so optimistic as there had been considerable rain in the area through the winter and spring, but the SCTA still identified four courses that could be prepared and, even though damp, the salt was drying out nicely when they began grooming the tracks. Even one week out from Speed Week things were looking good and teams began their treks to the mecca of speed racing with some confidence it would be another good meeting. And then it rained again, only a few days before the meeting was

due to start, and too late for most racers who were already on site or converging on Wendover. Still the organisers were confident it would dry out enough to get some racing underway early in the designated Speed Week, it just meant being patient and at least tech inspection and setting up of the pits could be done at a leisurely pace.

Despite the damp start, the access road to the pits wasn't badly affected, however areas of the pits were quite slushy and wet, especially on the Friday and Saturday. Weather forecasts were for not particularly hot weather and reasonable breezes, so the salt started to dry out remarkably well and by Sunday afternoon the SCTA announced racing

ABOVE: Classic sixties/seventies style T bucket looks right at home on the salt where you don't need front brakes anyway!

ABOVE RIGHT: The impromptu show at the Golden Nugget casino car park is always a highlight of Bonneville Speed Week. Typical attendees are traditional styled rods like this chopped '32 Ford three window coupe with tri-power Caddy engine owned by Doug Drake from Nevada.
RIGHT: The Karmann Ghia of the Mursick/Weigand "I Scream Inc." Racing Team ran in H/CGALT class where they posted a best speed of 119.235 mph.
BELOW: Wet salt makes for great group photos while there isn't much racing going on. This group is from the Denver Deton8ers. From left to right they are RJ Barnes' Deuce coupe, Todd Read's '30 Model A coupe, Clint Glasgow's '31 Model A coupe and Ed Gallagher's '28 Model A roadster.

would commence on Tuesday morning with all competitors using the long course only and the track shortened to a maximum of six miles. While the announcement of some racing was welcome, it was evident we were not going to see much racing from the really fast streamliners that need all of the track to reach their goals. Racing was to be on a first-in-line first-to-race basis with no pre-staging, so there were going to be long lines and plenty of waiting, but at least they would have the chance to race.

Meanwhile the usual car show at the Nugget Casino kept everyone occupied in the evenings where the array of interesting, clever and yes, even ridiculous cars lined up and stories of the past were relived by the large crowds.

The damp course didn't last long and by mid-afternoon Tuesday racing was halted as several cars spun out, so the SCTA decided the course needed to be moved over for a new racing surface on the Wednesday. It was already evident that this would be the story for the remainder of Speed Week, so several teams called it quits and packed up. Although a few entries made it into impound on those first couple of days only 25 records were set and Speed Week 2019 went into the books as one that didn't quite work out like most had hoped.

ABOVE LEFT & LEFT: Check out the wild banger four cylinder engine in the Hannemann Fiberglass '32 coupe. It has been fitted with an OHV conversion and fuel injection.
ABOVE RIGHT: Fenderless '33 Ford roadster is a tidy piece that has been given the patina treatment and sports a dressed flathead V8 engine.
BELOW: Looking like perfection in motion, the Speed Demon pushes off for one of several attempts to set new records. Poor track conditions meant few of the top end racers reached their goals this year.

ABOVE LEFT: Super looking chopped '50 Ford coupe looks right at home on the salt – complete with lakes pipes!
LEFT: Cut down Model A lakester style street rod caught everyone's attention with clever engineering that saw the engine block used as a stressed member of the chassis. Bonneville is the place to go to see such clever engineering.

ABOVE: The McFaddin, Lloyd, Gray Camaro made one run with a top speed of 178.385 mph on the shortened course while the Studebaker waited in vain for the course to get better.

ABOVE RIGHT: Overhead photo from the top of the Golden Nugget casino car park gives a different angle on the Rolling Bones-built chopped '34 Ford coupe of George Poteet and '32 Ford Tudor of Juy Watson.

RIGHT: Looking like a couple of bandits, this pair protect themselves from getting burnt while trekking up and down the spectator area in their Jeep.

ABOVE RIGHT: Quad Stromberg 97 carbs on a Chrysler Hemi engine give this '33 Ford three window coupe a sense of purpose. Mercury caps on painted steel wheels and Patina paint on the body all add to the overall image.

ABOVE: Quad carbs again, this time on a small block Ford engine in this dappled '30 Model A Ford hiboy coupe that's been chopped and equipped with twin side pipes in typical lakes fashion.

ABOVE: Looking like a bullet fired from a gun, the Albion Arrow streamliner heads off on its only run, a 146.768 mph effort.

ABOVE: Hard to imagine how you could make a Datsun coupe any more streamlined than the Team McLeish H/GCC version that only successfully completed one run at 144.792 mph.

ABOVE: Kevin Bradburn's '46 Harley Davidson competed in the 1350 AVG class. Kevin made several runs, with a best of 110.914 mph.

LEFT: Beautiful Chet Thomas blown street roadster has 493 cubic inch Ford engine that ran a best speed of 194.963 mph in the first quarter mile!

ABOVE: At first glance you might think this is a '32 Ford pickup but its actually a Chevy, scooting along at speed on the access road out to the salt racing.

ABOVE: Lucky Burton's beautiful and radically chopped '30 Model A Ford competition coupe appears to have stayed in the pits as there was no recorded speed for it in 2019.

LEFT: There was a lot of anticipation as the Team Vesco Turbinator II lined up on the start line only to lose power and have to be pushed away. A later run was also aborted before the turbine powered monster reached the first of the timers.

BELOW: Is it 2019 or 1949? This hiboy Deuce roadster has all the attributes of an early salt racer including the number on the door. There's no mistaking the profile of the flathead engine.

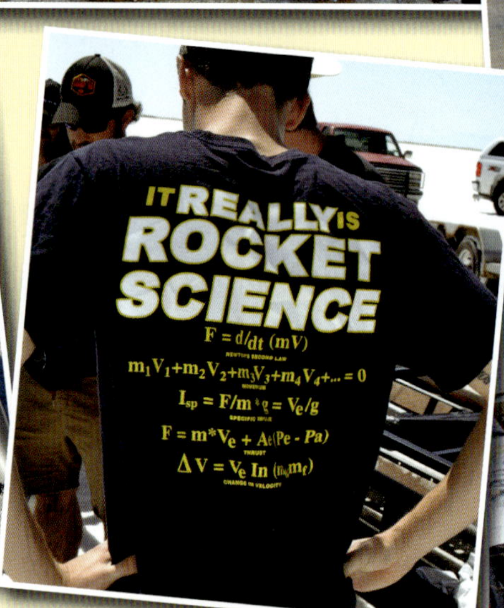

LEFT: Another Chrysler Hemi powered retro rod, this time a '33 Ford three window coupe with mandatory salt spatter and black painted wheels with blackwall tyres. It belongs to Kipp Winward.

BELOW: Characters abound in equally character filled hot rods at Bonneville. This '27 Model T tourer has the right accessory to fend off the Utah sun – a large umbrella - not speed tested though!

BELOW LEFT: Diminutive streamliner actually qualifies as a motorcycle side car outfit and usually enjoys considerable success. The Nebulous Theorum VIII of Costella, Cunha and Bassano used 1000cc Suzuki for power to go 164.274 mph on a qualifying run, 190.754 on the return for a final new record of 177.514 mph.

ABOVE CENTRE: Just in case you weren't sure what it takes to be successful at salt lake racing – here's the equation!

RIGHT: There's always something different and interesting in the Golden Nugget car park. Check out this wildly tubbed and caged Escort (Prefect to Aussies) wagon.

BELOW: Racers came from all parts of the world to compete at Bonneville Speed Week 2019. Serhii Malyk brought his electric motorcycle from the Ukraine, only to suffer no-go problems right on the start line during his first run.

www.graffitipub.com.au

TOP: There's always lots of action around the 911 roadster as it prepares for a run. This year the fearsome roadster had to be content with a best speed of 243.706 mph in B/BFMR class.

ABOVE: Reading the backs of overalls and T shirts can be quite entertaining at this event.

ABOVE: Brian Thomas has been driving his low-riding Model A based bucket out here for Speed Week for years. Outstanding engineering and individual styling are his trademarks.

BELOW: It was only on display but the Mooneyes "Jocko" streamliner and its matching towing rig certainly attracted a lot of attention when parked on the salt.

TOP: "Tumbleweed Racers" Crew Chief Ayu Yamakita prepares Kevin Bradburn's 1350cc 1946 Harley Davidson motorcycle at the start of Speed Week.

TOP RIGHT: Japanese competitor Kyo Kat ran his 175cc Honda in M-G class, making only one run at 55.353 mph.

ABOVE: Even amongst the officials you will find members from outside America. At left is Bob Ellis from the DLRA in Australia who is a regular volunteer at Speed Week Tech Inspections.

ABOVE RIGHT: UK Competitor Bill Cleyndert shipped his E/GAS lakester over and ran 200.721 mph.

RIGHT: Slick looking motorcycle ventured over from Grosseto, Italy. Dino Luciano's OED Racing Team used 1000cc Triumph power to go 126.208 mph.

BELOW: Derek Thomasen is a New Zealander who competed in his '31 Model A Ford coupe with original banger power going 72.781 mph.

LEFT: Chris Bridgewater has a 3000cc S&S engine in his Winks/LSD motorcycle that powered him to a best speed of 152.238 mph.

RIGHT: Another team from New Zealand was the Cook Motor Racing Team with their 2000cc Nissan powered streamliner that didn't make a pass and their G/GALT coupe that went 131.903 mph.

BELOW RIGHT: Bertrand Dubet is a French competitor who went 169.704 mph on his 1350cc Salt and Copper Aprilia motorcycle.

BELOW: This racer was built in New Zealand but Craig Johnson now races out of Washington state. He's in the line up to the start here but we can't find any recorded speed for the car.

BOTTOM: This was the scene that greeted racers on arrival in the pits at Bonneville. The salt had been reported as very good until heavy rain on the Wednesday leading up to Speed Week turned the salt to mush. Racing was delayed from Saturday until Tuesday morning but was only conducted over three shortened days on shortened courses that had to be moved across each day. Many opted to turn around and go home or sit out the week hoping for conditions to get better, but ultimately few got to make meaningful runs.

ABOVE: A Belgian visitor this time. Maurice DeBriffe fitted his sleek racer with a 984cc Harley Davidson engine but no recorded run is shown in the results.

LEFT: There's no place like Bonneville to see amazing engineering and racing car design. This green streamliner shows the extremes of aerodynamic design.
ABOVE: Why not use a Rolls Royce to tow your F100 race car? Black Creek Racing went 105.178 mph in XF/BFMP.

RIGHT: Bonneville attracts a wide range of enthusiast vehicles of all type - whether racing or not! Steve Darnell gets a bird's eye view of the pits from his bare metal 1968 Charger, "Overcharged". It's mounted on a 4×4 1-ton chassis and runs twin 6-71 superchargers and two turbochargers on a 5.9 litre Cummins inline-six.

BELOW RIGHT: Rustic Model T tourer looked like it would be a ton of fun to ramble about in. The banger engine had been dressed up with Cragar OHV conversion and twin carbs feeding through a side mounted blower.

BELOW: The Golden Nugget Casino car park show in the evenings creates its own atmosphere that is hard to describe. Let's just say it feels good!

MAIN PIC: Shiny streamliner of the Eddie's Chop Shop Team sets off from the start line on damp salt but still managed a best speed of 228.148mph in B/BGS class.

LEFT: Overhead shot of this hiboy '34 Ford roadster makes you want to jump in and drive it!

BELOW FAR LEFT: Dean Vanuttini took in Bonneville as part of his USA adventure in his flamed '33 Ford coupe, all the way from Melbourne, Australia and straight from the NSRA Nationals in Louisville, Kentucky.

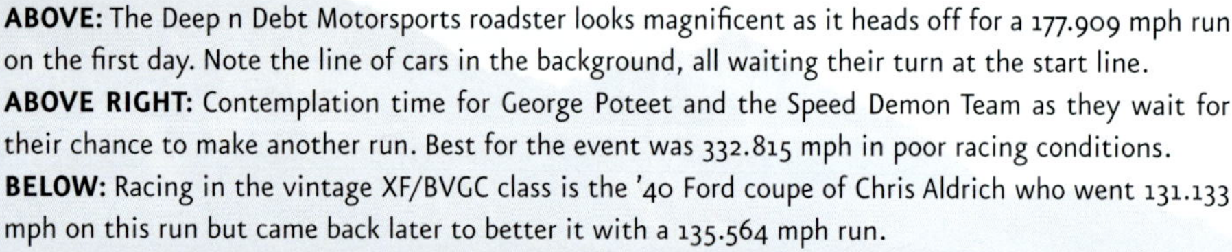

ABOVE: The Deep n Debt Motorsports roadster looks magnificent as it heads off for a 177.909 mph run on the first day. Note the line of cars in the background, all waiting their turn at the start line.
ABOVE RIGHT: Contemplation time for George Poteet and the Speed Demon Team as they wait for their chance to make another run. Best for the event was 332.815 mph in poor racing conditions.
BELOW: Racing in the vintage XF/BVGC class is the '40 Ford coupe of Chris Aldrich who went 131.133 mph on this run but came back later to better it with a 135.564 mph run.

ABOVE: Sleek looking entry of the Guthrie-Levie Racing Team actually qualifies as a motorcycle, racing in the SCS/BF class using a 2000cc engine. Best speed was 147.347 mph.

ABOVE RIGHT: Hot rods and white salt make a perfect combination as seen by this pair, '30 Model A Ford coupe at left and flathead powered channelled '32 Ford roadster on the right that belongs to Keven from the Revs Car Club.

RIGHT: There's 403 cubic inches of puffed diesel engine in the '54 Chevy truck of Pilgrim & Stubbs C/DT out of Rockport, Texas. Results don't show any runs being made this year as many elected not to venture from the pits in the vain hope that conditions might get better.

NEW RECORDS 2019

Entry No.	Name	Engine	Body	Qualifying	Return	New Record	Driver
181	Mursick Weigand	H	CGALT	119.235	113.111	116.173	Z. Davidson
672	Salty Frog Racing	G	DT	152.949	152.454	152.701	E. Persson
853	Black Creek Racing	XF	BFMP	105.178	102.696	103.937	D. Panich
890	Allan Burns	XXF	VOT	145.627	144.693	145.160	A. Burns
1616	Redneck Rocket	E	BFMMP	98.477	99.721	99.099	M. Collins
3201	Bonneville Bugeye	G	GMS	180.753	183.536	182.144	W. Iliff
3259	Chris Aldrich	XO	BGR	151.837	148.354	150.095	D. Aldrich
4884	Scrap Iron II	XF	BFALT	141.841	143.804	142.822	P. Landry
169B	John Stoner LSR	350CC	MPS-VBF	68.642	70.659	69.650	Velocette
286B	La Bandida Racing	125CC	MPS-BF	54.508	56.692	55.600	Honda
555B	Foley and Eller Racing	1650CC	SC-VG	106.203	92.384	99.293	H/D
586B	Puckett LSR	350CC	MPS-PBF	78.595	84.453	81.524	BSA
602B	Corey Bertelsen	250CC	SC-BF	76.848	77.094	76.646	Yamaha
654B	Bridgewater LSR	3000CC	A-PBF	152.238	157.491	154.864	Rolling Thunder
674B	Arkansas Speed Society	125CC	MPS-BG	68.431	67.217	67.824	Honda
760B	Team McLeish RS	125CC	MPS-BF	96.832	95.444	96.138	Honda
903B	Arkansas Speed Society	125CC	MPS-BG	63.500	61.186	62.343	Honda
1113B	Tim Tim Racing	50CC	MPS-PBG	40.796	41.113	40.954	Honda
1115B	Puckett LSR	100CC	SC-BF	50.025	56.467	53.246	Honda
1304B	Baxters Benelli	250CC	SC-PBG	27.726	31.465	29.595	Beuelli
1602B	Corey Bertelsen	250CC	SC-BG	78.728	65.025	71.876	Yamaha
1712B	Don Q Racing RBM	100CC	A-PG	49.311	52.002	50.656	Honda
2107B	The Red Baron LSR	350CC	MPS-PBF	111.160	100.032	105.596	Moridi
4220B	Ian Arnold	100CC	SC-BG	57.967	57.263	57.615	Arnold
8080B	Costella/Cunha/Bassano Nebulous T	1000CC	SCS-BG	164.274	190.754	177.514	Costella/Cunha

PROFILE: Lloyd Wilson – Magoo's Street Rods, Masterton New Zealand

Lloyd Wilson grew up in Levin, a small town famous for its motor racing circuit, where he got to meet a lot of the great world renowned and local competitors. "Red Dawson was my hero, he drove a Mustang, my favourite vehicle at the time. I even had a slot car based on his car". One day Lloyd called into his local tuck shop where he found a magazine that had Red Dawson's Mustang on the cover. He bought it and instantly got his introduction to hot rodding. As it happened, two days later a hot rod that was featured in the magazine turned up in Levin, so he actually got to see it in the metal.

"I thought that was pretty cool. To go racing was too expensive and I was only 15 so it wasn't viable to have a race car, but with hot rodding you could work your way into it a piece at a time."

Lloyd's mother worked in a dress shop, where the son of the owner had pocket size Rod & Custom, and Car Illustrated magazines and these helped germinate the seed in him as Lloyd's dad wasn't a car guy at all.

"I decided to get into building a hot rod, but didn't know what was involved and there was no help from home. My education was purely academic – my childhood ambition was to be a lawyer and I had no exposure to the enthusiast car world." Contact with a club was the best option but there was no hot rod club in Lloyd's town, so the 15 year old teenager decided to start a club and, not yet even having a drivers licence, rode his bicycle all over town to see anyone who was remotely interested in cars. The inaugural meeting of Tararua Rodders was soon convened. His interest really kicked off from that first meeting and he soon purchased and started work on a '38 Ford Standard coupe that was converted to a '37. It was followed by an F100 pickup, then a '32 Ford roadster that Lloyd kept for a number of years. Next came a '32 Ford Fordor project that was more suited to a family.

In 1997 the business officially started. In the process of importing parts for his own projects, and frustrated by unreliable panel beaters, others asked if Lloyd could bring parts in for them, so he gradually turned the hobby into a business. A local panelbeater was tired of working on normal cars and was looking to work in a more satisfying job. Lloyd made an agreement with him to get some work booked in and set up properly in business so he would come work for Lloyd. At that time Lloyd also employed an engineer and Magoo's Street Rods was officially up and running. In New Zealand most hot rodders have nick-names. Because he used to wear glasses, Lloyd was given the title "Magoo", so it was natural to roll this into the business.

Lloyd leased a building that was suddenly sold without warning, so he set up in a specially built workshop at home and hired a couple more guys. The business quickly outgrew that site, so Magoo's was moved to its own purpose-built shop in a Masterton industrial area. That was 13 years ago and since then the business has completed almost 50 turn key rods, plus multiple roller vehicles. Currently there are 27 vehicles under construction in the workshop and the work comes from all around New Zealand. Magoo's has even done work for Kiwis living overseas. The shop is predominantly known for pre '49 projects, especially '32 Fords, but also caters for street machines, classics, and restorations.

The philosophy of the business is "We build nice cars, for nice people". The team of seven handle engineering, bodywork and fabrication, wiring, including audio installs, upholstery, and paint preparation in-house.

ABOVE: Days like this make it all the hard work worth it - cruising California with two of my good friends over there; Mike Gialdini and John Casubolo.

ABOVE LEFT: Instead of attending University Entrance accrediting in my 6th form high school year I played hooky and headed off to Taupo with friends to attend the 1st NZ Street Rod Nationals.

ABOVE: Lloyd leads a group of Deuces during the New Zealand Deuce Days Run that was held in Masterton in March 2019. Lloyd was the main organiser of the event. The three window coupe is flathead powered and uses one of Magoo's own fibreglass repro bodies.

LEFT: On the left is Lloyd's wife Anne's '34 Ford Tudor that has been a long-term project but now almost finished. The chopped '30 Model A Ford pickup was built for Todd and Julie Smyth and was featured on the cover of the April issue 2019 New Zealand Hot Rod Magazine. The pickup features Ford running gear right through, based on a 302 Windsor engine.

Magoo's were buying their fibreglass bodies from Deuce Farm, but the owner wanted to get out of the business and Lloyd needed to maintain supply and quality control, so he purchased the moulds and brought the process in-house. Since then Magoo's has added the '34 Ford five window coupe body and they redid the '32 Ford five window body mould. Currently they manufacture the '32 Ford five window coupe, '32 Ford three window coupe, '32 Ford roadster and the '34 Ford five window coupe. All are fully assembled, hinged and latched to New Zealand's LVVTA standards.

Chassis are mostly fabricated using imported American Stamping rails and built in-house to the New Zealand standards. All are built in jigs and individually engineered according to the customer's specifications for that build. Magoo's is one of the New Zealand agent for all leading US brands, so components vary according to customer requirements using US based and local suppliers.

There are four different grades of work undertaken at Magoo's; turn key cars, rollers, supply the body and parts to the customer and they assemble their own chassis, and piece work on street rods and customs – accident repair, engine transplant etc.

The list of Lloyd's own cars includes the already mentioned '37 Ford coupe that had 289 V8 running gear and the F100 with stock 272 engine. This was Lloyd's courting vehicle when he and wife, Anne were dating and she remained patient when there were breakdowns, proving she was the right girl for Lloyd. Then came the '32 Ford roadster that did lots of miles but wasn't practical once the family arrived. The '32 Fordor sedan was more suited, even with its chopped roof and it was to be a hiboy, but they shifted house with a growing family so it was sold. There were a couple more incomplete Model A projects and then a Model A Tudor that was converted to a sedan delivery and became the trademark of the business for many years. It was used as family transport and travelled extensively to events, even winning a national award for Best Participating Family. The delivery is now in Western Australia where it still sees regular use with a new owner. A '34 Ford Tudor for Anne was planned as a daily runner and was included as part of setting up the business. The theory was to work on customers' cars part of the week and the '34 one day of the week, but it didn't work out, so 20 years later the '34 is still going together. It is very close to finished now. On the bucket list for Lloyd is a '39 Ford Deluxe coupe and a '36 Ford roadster. He is sure he will own both at some time in the future.

In the meantime Lloyd completed a '32 Ford three window coupe for himself. It has become well known throughout New Zealand and features traditional hiboy styling with flathead running gear. A Buick nailhead powered '30 Model A roadster-pickup is also in the current crop of rods, but it is kept in America, where it acted as the push car for Bill Ward's Bonneville racer in 2008. From there Lloyd drove it directly to Pleasanton for the Goodguys' West Coast Nationals where it won the coveted Stroker McGurk Award. Lloyd continues to use the Model A pickup when he is in the USA. There's one more current project for Lloyd – this one is his dream car and it is well under way in the workshop, another '32 Ford roadster with injected Hemi and bright red paint scheme.

Lloyd offered these observations when asked about the future of hot rodding in New Zealand. "Much has changed since I first started in hot rodding – obviously it has become more expensive and there are fewer young people involved, not just because of the cost – the younger generations don't relate so much to the hot rod era cars, but we do still get some younger customers and there is still growth in the hobby. That growth often comes from the people now in their forties and older, looking for toy as a reward after rearing families and establishing businesses etc. Our oldest customer is 77 but that is still younger than many enthusiasts in the USA. The NZ based hobby will be stable for the next 20 years. The Low Volume Vehicle scheme had some faults in the development phase, but maintains our ability to keep pursuing our hobby. We can even have fenderless hiboys etc.

ABOVE: Always time for a chat with customers in the retail shop.
BELOW: Magoo's stocks everything from whole bodies to parts and books.

ABOVE: One of Magoo's own '32 Ford five window bodies awaits a buyer.
BELOW: This time it's a reproduction fibreglass '32 Ford roadster just waiting to be mated to a Magoo's built chassis.

ABOVE INSET: Wife Anne has been an important part of the ride for the last 40 years.

ABOVE: Lloyd organised the New Zealand Deuce Days event in his home town of Masterton in March 2019, so it made sense to have entrants come to the shop for registration.

BELOW: The workshop is departmentalised for efficient operations. Here we have a '38 Chevy sedan in the mechanical building section.

ABOVE: A fresh out of the mould '32 three window coupe sits on a chassis, ready to become part of another street rod project.

BELOW: Magoo's even have a '31 Ford Vicky repro body in their product line. This one is in primer and well on the way to completion.

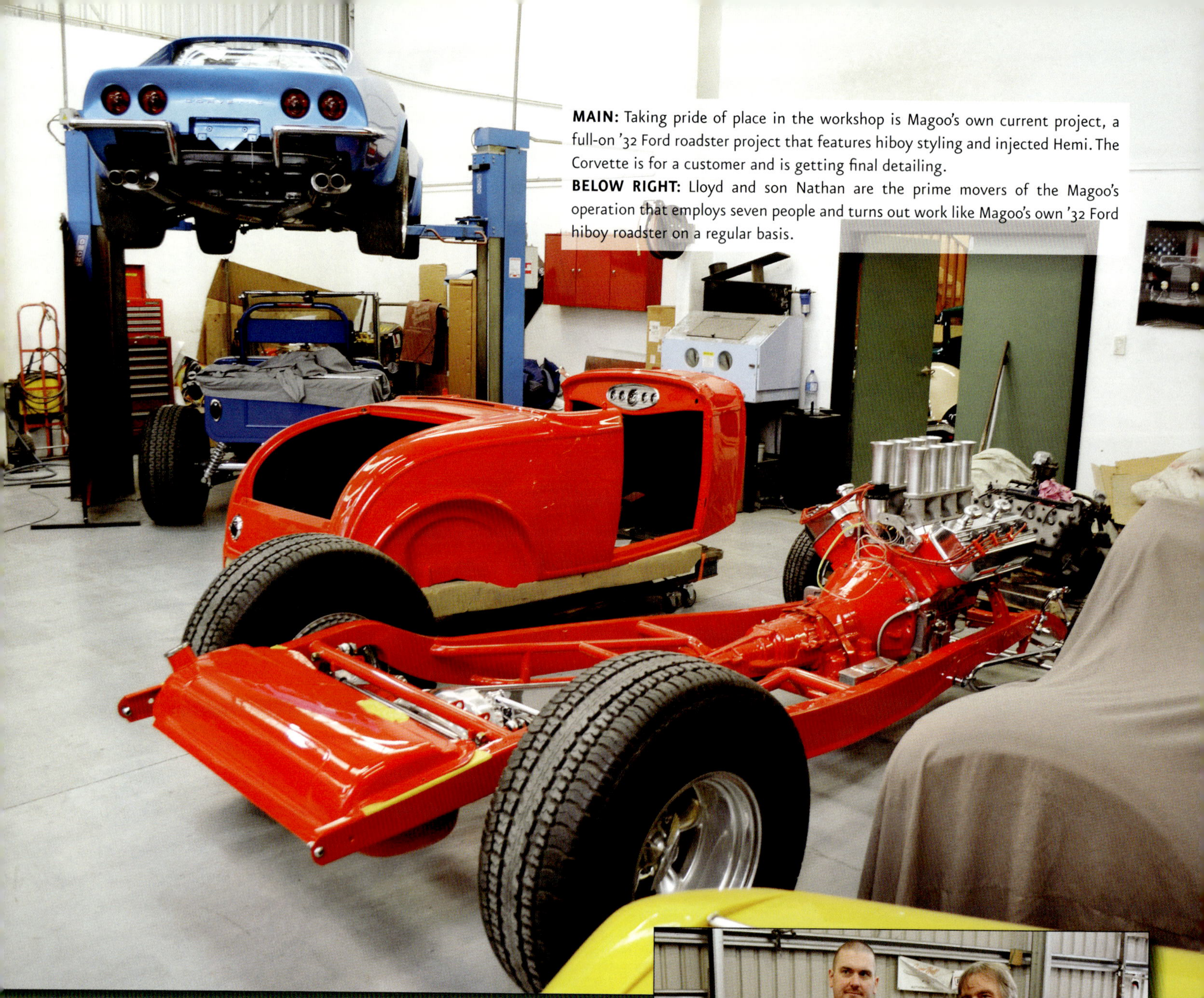

MAIN: Taking pride of place in the workshop is Magoo's own current project, a full-on '32 Ford roadster project that features hiboy styling and injected Hemi. The Corvette is for a customer and is getting final detailing.

BELOW RIGHT: Lloyd and son Nathan are the prime movers of the Magoo's operation that employs seven people and turns out work like Magoo's own '32 Ford hiboy roadster on a regular basis.

BELOW: From this angle you can see the diff flange mounted alternator, built in driveshaft safety loop and high quality overall finish. The roadster is in the final stages of assembly.

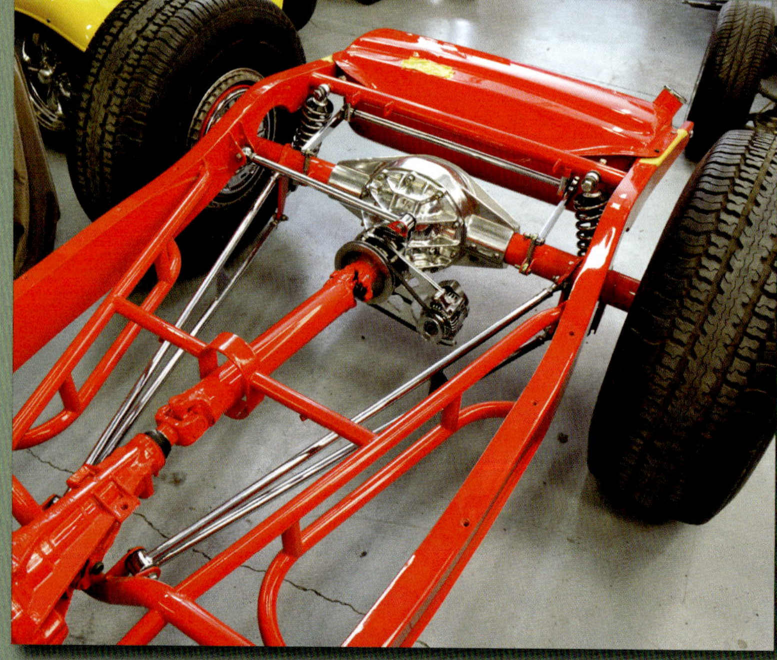

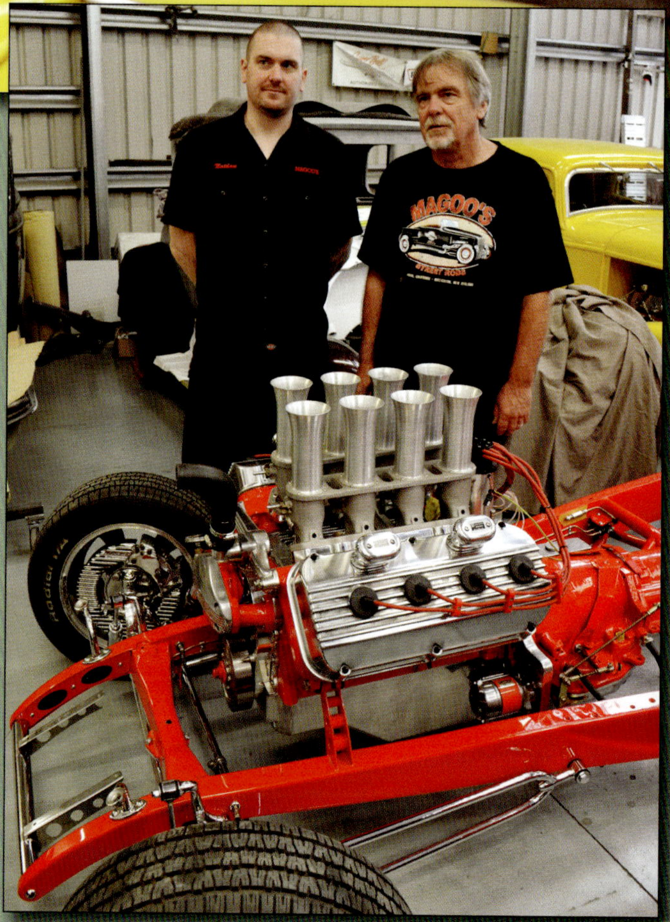

with certain limitations. The process has given people the confidence to invest in the cars as a result of setting up this LVVTA system.

I think we will see more trends toward street machine type projects. We are now a lot closer to the standards of the US cars and we continue to be influenced by them. The average New Zealand rodder uses his or her car for more than just events and now we have an excess of options for events, an incredible range of choices. This hurts the big national events but has accelerated the public exposure to, and interest in, hot rodding, as do the 'reality' TV car programmes". ■

ABOVE: The '32 Fordor project the day it was chopped.
TOP RIGHT: Anne cruising in the '30 Model A pickup with Lloyd at Pleasanton.
ABOVE RIGHT: The original Magoo's company vehicle, now in Australia.
RIGHT: Sitting in the final assembly area of the shop and almost ready for delivery is a '32 Ford three window coupe finished in bright yellow and equipped with Ford running gear.
BELOW: They all start from the very basics as you can see with this fibreglass reproduction five window coupe and '48 Ford chassis that has been treated to an increased step up over the rear end.
BELOW INSET: Up in the loft is a '30 Model A Ford coupe body that is destined to become a street rod project for another family member, this one is for Daniel.

BELOW: Two more of the high quality shop projects at Magoo's. The pickup on the left is a '46 Chevy that is well under way. The superbly finished two tone '65 Pontiac convertible has been fully rebuilt from end to end for the Auckland based owner.

BELOW: Blue '32 five window coupe is a Magoo's fibreglass repro with chopped top and in gel-coat finish ready to go on its chassis.

BOTTOM: Another future personal project for Magoo is this '27 Model T Ford tourer that waits its turn in Lloyd's home workshop where the business started out. These days it houses his own collection of cars and memorabilia.

BELOW: More projects under way in the workshop. In the foreground we have a steel '32 Ford roadster that is being built old-timey style while the '48 Ford coupe body in the background is in hi-fill primer.

BOTTOM: My first Deuce roadster at the Ashburton Street Rods Nats in the early 1980s.

ABOVE: During the Deuce Days Run, entrants made a visit to Magoo's home workshop to check out some of his past and future projects, plus memorabilia.

ABOVE: One of Lloyd's prized possessions is an original Dragmaster Dart FED that was owned and raced by Mickey Thompson.

ABOVE LEFT INSET: In amongst the projects at the home workshop is son, Nathan's Cal style Volkswagen beetle that awaits its turn to go back on the road.

ABOVE RIGHT INSET: Lloyd was a foundation member of Tararua Rodders and was awarded this Foundation Member medallion in appreciation of his work in getting the club established. These days he is a member of Oceanside Rodders.

ABOVE: The 1300 square metre workshop is departmentalised for different stages of the custom car building process and has a retail shop at the front. For the 2019 Deuce Days Rod Run it was also used as the registration point for entrants.

LEFT: Here's an old photo back to when I was 16 and working on my first coupe. Each of those back tires took a few weeks of pocket money from after school jobs to purchase!

32nd ANNUAL
FLASHBACK
Classic Car Show

Glendora, California, USA
Glendora Kiwanis Club & Glendora Chamber of Commerce

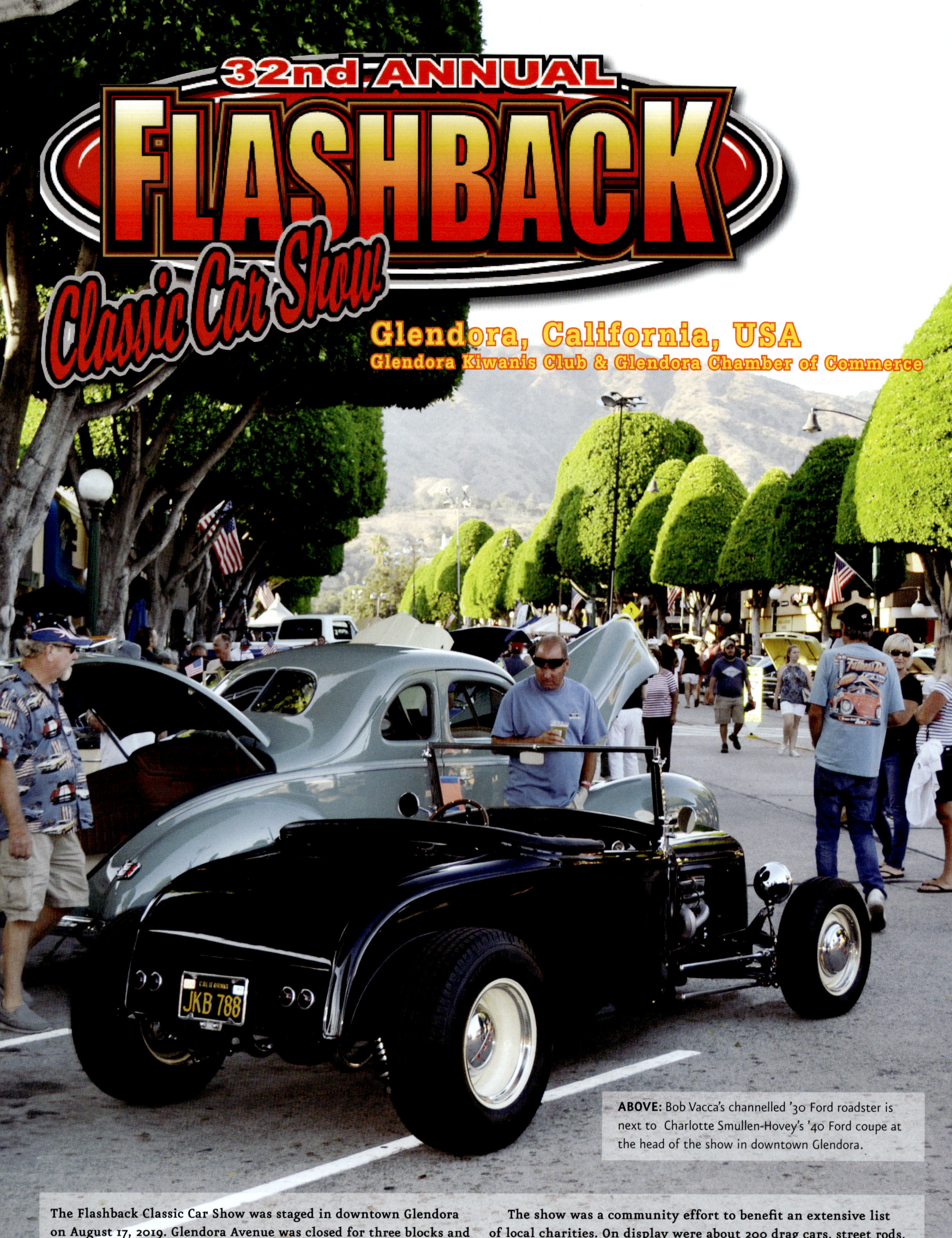

ABOVE: Bob Vacca's channelled '30 Ford roadster is next to Charlotte Smullen-Hovey's '40 Ford coupe at the head of the show in downtown Glendora.

The Flashback Classic Car Show was staged in downtown Glendora on August 17, 2019. Glendora Avenue was closed for three blocks and temporary lighting installed to brighten up the show area. Local groups assisted, food vans and cafes were open and bands played.

The show was a community effort to benefit an extensive list of local charities. On display were about 200 drag cars, street rods, customs, muscle cars – and one tractor! The show enjoyed very good public support in a perfect venue on a balmy summer evening.

ABOVE & BELOW: Steve & Melanie McKinney's '60 Chevy Impala has nicely dressed 409 engine and low stance thanks to air suspension.

ABOVE, BELOW & RIGHT: Craig Stewart from San Gabriel is the third owner of this superb Plymouth Fury. It has 47,400 original miles on the clock and still has its original space inspired steering wheel. Every piece of polished trim is in perfect condition.

ABOVE & RIGHT: Kerry Morris' Chevy pickup shares space with Jim St Pierre's flamed '40 Chevy coupe in the foreground.

LEFT: Nick Nicassio's '60 Ford Starliner is a classic example of a breed not often seen any more.

BELOW: Tony Rosella's 1937 Ford coupe has mile deep Chamelion paint that flips from purple to blue depending on your viewing angle.

BELOW LEFT: We don't often see the smaller Mercury Comets of the early fifties era as customs and this example was really well done.

ABOVE: The classic lines of the '57 Buick hardtop look best from three quarter rear.

ABOVE: Two tone Chevy pickup with the colours separated by a line of flames looks outstanding.

ABOVE: Darrell Moyer's Chevy 3100 has been in the family for over 50 years. It has been chopped 3-1/2 inches, runs a 383 stoker with 750 Holley carby and ceramic coated headers. The pickup is painted in HOK Cortez Blue with ghost flames and graphics.
LEFT: Mike Lambert's Chevy delivery is outfitted in typical fashion for the era as a specialty baker's van.

LEFT: Jim Rosenberger's Chevy wagon mixes all three year models with '55 front, '56 rear and '57 side trim, very clever and done so well it looks factory.
BELOW: Tregg Wright's satin black Olds S-8 won Best Modified Custom 1949-73.

ABOVE: Charles Tachdjian's 1956 Ford F100 big window pickup was designed, built and maintained by BOBCO. Features include a Camaro front clip, GM Performance crate ZZ4, 700R4 transmssion, Ford nine inch rear, power brakes, Ron Mangus interior, oak bed, and Boyd Coddington Wheels.

RIGHT: Swoopy '34 Ford roadster of John Buck is channelled and stylised with louvred three piece hood. It is powered by a Roush 351 Ford engine and has Ron Mangus interior trim done in beige leather.

ABOVE: John Kennedy's Chevy Biscayne sits right and exhibits a high standard of finish to its white painted bodywork set off by aqua painted steel wheels.

ABOVE: Phil Lee's radically channelled '32 Ford pickup sports Model A wheels and grille plus a honkin' small block Chevy V8 engine.

FAR LEFT: Yes, there was even a tractor in the show! Roger Hahn's tri-wheel beauty is a 1952 McCormick Farmall Super C.

LEFT: John Kennedy also owns this Cj7 Jeep that was built for style and purpose. Big wheels, a full roll cage and Chevy Vortec V8 running gear means there is nowhere this fun ride would be uncomfortable.

ABOVE: Ralph Sears' '36 Ford convertible is a desirable collector car made even better with the full street rod treatment and small block Chevy engine.

ABOVE: Jim Clark's '57 Studebaker pickup finished in bright yellow simply can't be ignored. Under the hood is a small bock Chevy V8 engine.

ABOVE: Joe Eddy's Blue '58 Chevy Impala sits alongside Joseph Santoro's Green & white '56 Chevy 210, graphically illustrating how much the Chevy design evolved in just two years.